THE MALINOIS

K9 Professional Training Series

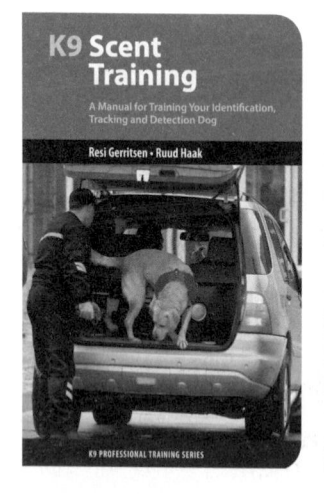

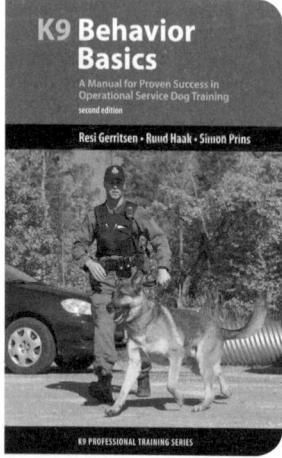

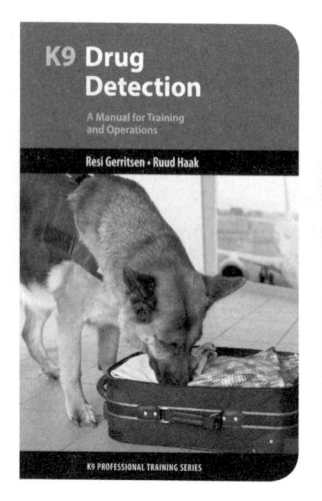

K9 Scent Training
A Manual for Training Your Identification, Tracking and Detection Dog
Resi Gerritsen • Ruud Haak

K9 Behavior Basics
A Manual for Proven Success in Operational Service Dog Training
second edition
Resi Gerritsen • Ruud Haak • Simon Prins

K9 Search and Rescue
A Manual for Training the Natural Way
second edition
Resi Gerritsen • Ruud Haak

K9 Drug Detection
A Manual for Training and Operations
Resi Gerritsen • Ruud Haak

K9 Explosive and Mine Detection
A Manual for Training and Operations
Resi Gerritsen • Ruud Haak

K9 Schutzhund Training
A Manual for IPO Training through Positive Reinforcement
second edition
Resi Gerritsen • Ruud Haak

See the complete list at
dogtrainingpress.com

THE MALINOIS

The History and Development of the Breed in Schutzhund, Detection, and Police Work

Dr. Resi Gerritsen
Ruud Haak

K9 Professional Working Breeds Series

An imprint of
Brush Education Inc.

Copyright © 2018 Resi Gerritsen and Ruud Haak

18 19 20 21 22 5 4 3 2 1

Thank you for buying this book and for not copying, scanning, or distributing any part of it without permission. By respecting the spirit as well as the letter of copyright, you support authors and publishers, allowing them to continue to create and distribute the books you value.

Excerpts from this publication may be reproduced under licence from Access Copyright, or with the express written permission of Brush Education Inc., or under licence from a collective management organization in your territory. All rights are otherwise reserved, and no part of this publication may be reproduced, stored in a retrieval system, or transmitted in any form or by any means, electronic, mechanical, photocopying, digital copying, scanning, recording, or otherwise, except as specifically authorized.

Brush Education Inc.
www.brusheducation.ca
contact@brusheducation.ca

Editorial: Meaghan Craven
Index: Judy Dunlop
Cover design: John Luckhurst; Cover image: Dog Training Center Oosterhout
Interior design: Carol Dragich, Dragich Design

Printed and manufactured in Canada

Library and Archives Canada Cataloguing in Publication
Gerritsen, Resi, author
The malinois : the history and development of the breed in Schutzhund, detection and police work / Dr. Resi Gerritsen, Ruud Haak. (K9 professional working breeds series)

Includes bibliographical references and index.
Issued in print and electronic formats.
ISBN 978-1-55059-732-5 (softcover).—ISBN 978-1-55059-735-6 (EPUB).—
ISBN 978-1-55059-733-2 (PDF).—ISBN 978-1-55059-734-9 (Kindle)

1. Belgian malinois. 2. Working dogs. I. Haak, Ruud, author II. Title.

SF429.B4G47 2018   636.737   C2018-900637-4
                                        C2018-900638-2

Contents

Introduction vii
1. A History of Sheepdogs 1
2. The Belgian Malinois 23
3. Working Malinois in the Netherlands 67
4. Behavior, Raising, and Training 93
5. The Malinois as Police Dog 112
6. The Malinois in Other Roles 153

Conclusion: A Lack of Character 188

Appendix: KNPV National Champions, 1946–2017 193

Notes 201

Bibliography 203

About the Authors 205

Index 209

Introduction

By the end of the 19th to the beginning of the 20th century, Belgian shepherd dogs (Belgische Herdershonden, in Flemish), including the short-haired Mechelse herder (Malinois, in French), had a ragtag collection of coat colors and coat varieties. To this point, these dogs had been crossed and bred without much thought put into their appearance. The most important selection standards for breeding at the time were character, temperament, stamina, and agility.

Belgian shepherd dogs traditionally specialized in working with goats and sheep, as well as performing other farm tasks, including guarding properties, people, and other animals. These dogs lived with the "ordinary" person, who could only afford a dog if he earned his meals in return. Belgian shepherds' services proved valuable to the farmers and shepherds of the Belgian and Dutch border regions, especially when it came to guarding the house and yard, and herding sheep. Hence, the dogs were carefully bred and selected for these tasks for many centuries. By the end of the 19th century, however, people other than farmers and shepherds began to interfere with these dogs. This period saw the rise of cynology, and the serious study of dogs drew the hard-working canines of the country into urban areas, where breeders molded them into the

Figure 0.01 Four Belgian shepherds of three coat textures. From right to left: the black long-haired Belgian sheepdog or Groenendael, the long-haired Belgian Tervueren, the wire-coat Belgian Laekenois, and the short-coat Belgian Malinois. (Shutterstock / cynoclub)

different varieties of separate Dutch and Belgian shepherds for the purpose of exhibition.

The names of the different varieties of Belgian shepherd dogs still remind us of the regions where they originally performed their duties, for they were named for the Belgian cities and villages of Groenendael, Malines, Laeken, and Tervueren. At the time these varieties were named there were still plenty of sheep on the farms, and there was a great interest in the working dogs. Farmers and shepherds continued to employ them, and dog lovers in Malines enjoyed the company of their good working dogs.

The cynological interest that emerged at the end of the 19th century meant a lot of excitement for everything dog. Today, however, we doubt that cynological practices related to the Belgian shepherd dogs were good for the breed. The cynologists saw the opportunity to transform—over only a few years—the rough worker into a beautiful dog. By exhibiting Belgian shepherds, people ensured that the main characteristic of the dogs became their appearance, a practice that would begin to dilute the working-dog qualities that had made these dogs valuable to rural people. Long-, short-, and rough-haired dogs were separated, and each variety was classified by its permitted coat colors, something that had been meaningless to the working people who had used these dogs for centuries. Farmers and shepherds simply bred the best dogs, regardless of coat and color.

Today, Belgian shepherd dogs are separated into four closely related varieties, with three coat types:

- The Belgian sheepdog (Groenendael): a long, straight, and abundant coat with a collarette around the neck. The Groenendael is completely black.
- The Belgian Tervueren: like the Groenendael, a long-haired dog. The color is gray with black overlay, or the more favored rich fawn to russet mahogany with black overlay (a requirement for the Malinois). The coat is characteristically double pigmented; the tip of each fawn hair is black. A black mask and a minimum of eight pigmented points is obligatory: black at both ears, both upper eyelids, both upper lips, and both under lips.
- The Belgian Laekenois: a rough, wire-haired coat. Unlike the long-haired Belgian shepherds, the coat on the Laekenois's head is also long. This harsh, wiry, dry, and straight coat is reddish fawn with black shading, principally on the muzzle and tail.
- The Belgian Malinois: a comparatively short, straight coat, hard enough to be weather resistant, with a dense undercoat. The coat should be very short on the head, ears, and lower legs. The hair is somewhat longer around the neck, where it forms a collarette, and on the tail and backs of the thighs. The basic coloring is rich fawn to mahogany, with black tips on the hairs giving an overlay appearance. Other colors are not allowed. The Malinois has a black mask and the same pigment points as the Tervueren. The

tips of the toes may be white, and a small white spot on the breastbone/prosternum is permitted, but should not extend to the neck. Other white markings are faulted.

Despite the dilution of the working-dog qualities inherent to the Groenendael, Tervueren, and Laekenois since the early 20th century, the Malinois continued to be used very intensively for guarding and police tasks, and is still one of the best working dogs, bar none. The Malinois is found more and more everywhere in the world in the service of the police, customs, and armed forces. In this book, we will introduce you to this exceptional working dog.

We wish to thank Theo Dijkman, editor-in-chief of the popular Dutch working dog magazine *Hondensport & Sporthonden* (http://www.hondensport.com), for his contributions in text and pictures to Chapter 3, Working Malinois in the Netherlands. And we also thank Sonja and Hans van Rossum for providing their beautiful photos.

–Dr. Resi Gerritsen and Ruud Haak

Disclaimer

While the contents of this book are based on substantial experience and expertise, working with dogs involves inherent risks, especially in dangerous settings and situations. Anyone using approaches described in this book does so entirely at his or her own risk, and both the author and publisher disclaim any liability for any injuries or other damage that may be sustained.

1

A History of Sheepdogs

Origins

The domestication of wild animals did not happen once and only in a single place. In earlier times, paleontologists and archaeologists believed that the dog descended from a small mammal, called *Miacis*, that about 60 million years ago lived in the environs of what are now parts of Asia, and this genus became the ancestor of the animals known today as canids: dogs, jackals, wolves, and foxes. By about 30 to 40 million years ago *Miacis* had evolved into the first true dog *Cynodictis*. This was a medium-size animal, longer than it was tall, with a long tail and a brushy coat. Over the millennia, *Cynodictis* gave rise to two branches, one in Africa and the other in Eurasia. The Eurasian branch was called *Tomarctus* and is believed to be the progenitor of wolves, dogs, and foxes.

In the 20th century it was widely believed that the dog (*Canis familiaris*) descended from wolves and especially the gray wolf (*Canis lupus*). Research from 2014, however, suggest that today's dog breeds may not have evolved from the gray wolf, at least not the kind of gray wolf that exists today. Instead, dogs and gray wolves share a common ancestor in an extinct wolf lineage that existed thousands of years ago.

Figure 1.01 Occurring worldwide, the wolf (*Canis lupus*) is a mammal in the Canidae family, a predator (order Carnivora). Multiple subspecies are distinguished, including some that are extinct.

Figure 1.02 The dog (*Canis lupus familiaris*) descends from an extinct species of wolf, related to the gray wolf—also known as the timber or western wolf—and to other subspecies, including the Eurasian wolf (*Canis lupus lupus*) shown in this photo.

Where people and wolves in their many varieties lived together, dogs were slowly produced as pets. People took young wolves out of their dens and raised them. Researchers have proven that because of their new habits and diet, these newly domesticated animals had a stunted growth, and only after a long time did the "adopted" wolves' descendants grow into larger animals.[1]

Evidence of contact between early humans and domesticated wolves has been found at archaeological sites in Europe where the skeletons of wolves (or early dogs) together with prehistoric human remains have been found. For example, at the beginning of the 21st century, a skull found in the 1860s in the Belgian caves of Goyet (Gesves) was identified as that of an approximately 31,700-year-old paleolithic dog. Analysis of mitochondrial DNA from the skull confirms that the individual was not a direct ancestor of modern dogs, but rather of an extinct side branch with significant genetic diversity.[2] At at the Mezin Wolf Camp in Ukraine, dating back 24,000 years, the large numbers of wolf remains and especially the characteristics of a one-year-old skull led to the conclusion that the wolf was in the process of domestication in that area.[3] However, early relations between farmers and wolves was not always friendly. Wolves preyed on other domestic animals and were often viewed with fear. So how did people undergo such a fundamental change as to bring wild dogs into their lives and raise them as pets and companions, as herding and protecting helpers?

This shift likely started with the characteristics of the wolf. All types of wolf are generally the same, phenotypically, likely because wolves' territories overlap, so there was a lot of intermating that homogenized the "look" of the wolf.

While people rely heavily on their sense of sight to move through the world, wolves champion their sense of smell, which leads them to their food. In general, wild canines are extremely shy, careful, and suspicious—extremely suspicious of anything unknown to them. Their instincts tell them they are stronger in groups, and the drive to stay in a pack keeps them together. As a pack, they hunt, kill, and eat their prey, and together they return home. Their instincts lead them to go out at night or at twilight. In addition to their phenomenal sense of smell, they have excellent hearing, as well as eyes that easily adjust to the dark—two desirable characteristics for working dogs.

Ancient wolves avoided humans as much as possible, but the many alluring scents and warmth of the fire at human camps attracted them. Abandoned campsites, or other places once inhabited by people, would have been replete with the scent of humans, and leftover food or bones would have carried the smell of human hands and saliva. Even today, hungry wolves are not picky about what they eat, and in fact, hunger emboldens them to approach human settlements. And so it was that meat waste became the bait that eventually seduced ancient wolves to go to human sites more and more during their daily food-finding missions. Gradually, shyness of humans faded as human odors became more familiar.

As wolves began to recognize human scent, they followed the urge to be in more regular contact with people. Younger wolves may have even submitted themselves to human society, giving up their packs to join human ones. Young cubs from deserted lairs would have been taken by hunters to their settlements, and these young animals would soon be used to living with people. During mating, these animals would perhaps leave their people, but they would return after the business was completed.

With people, wolves could count on food and warmth. Female wolves may thus have chosen human settlements for their lairs. People would have found such lairs harmless, as long as there was enough food about for the wolves to eat. Having wolves nearby,

Figure 1.03 A dog with her Tiriyó master in the interior of Suriname, 1964. The people acquired dogs via trade with other Indigenous Peoples in Brazil.

after all, benefited people too. Ancient humans had enemies, from neighboring communities looking for spoils to big predators looking for a meal. Wolves in proximity to humans would, through their behavior, warn the people of all kinds of dangers, and this built-in early warning system would have been very helpful to those in camp.

Research about how people treat wild animal babies, including studies of young wild wolves, suggests that integrating a tamed wild animal into a human group does not cause too many problems, as long as the animal is a pack animal.[4] Because the wild wolf was able to subject himself to the person he viewed as the dominant human in camp, the pack leader, some wild wolves began to follow human camps, which led to the kind of relationships we see between humans and dogs today.

As many early humans in Europe transitioned from nomadic hunter-gatherers to farmers and cattle breeders, permanent settlements arose. Because of this change, the relationship between humans and dogs also changed, with the dogs finding roles as helpers around farms. Thus, dogs became more and more a part of specific family groupings, and humans and dogs relied on one another more and more.

"WOLF BLOOD"

People seem to think that the older the breed of dog, the better or "purer" that dog must be. In his 1964 book, *Jubileumboek*, Dick M. Engel wrote: "The estimated 3000-year-old image of a seated dog found at excavations in Assiout (Egypt) already shows a striking resemblance to a German shepherd." This sounds impressive, but if you think the ancestors of the present German shepherd dog guarded ancient pharaohs, you are fooling yourself. There is no conclusive evidence linking the two dogs. In fact, the Egyptian image was probably of a prototype of the extant Pharaohound—although even a modern geneticist could not likely untangle this breed to create the dogs of Egypt's former rulers.

In his 1923 book about the German shepherd, *The German Shepherd Dog in Word and Picture*, Max von Stephanitz spent more than 100 pages on a discussion of the dog's origin, claiming the breed descended from a prehistoric dog whose remains were found in Moscow and was called *Canis poutiatini*. Both Engel and Stephanitz claimed the present German shepherd descends from this animal, and they went into detail on the differences between it and the wolf. And this is the crux of the issue for both men: if it could be shown that the descendants of the shepherd dog and those of the wolf had nothing to do with each other, the serious threat to the breed—the assertion that it descended from wolves—could be combatted.

Figure 1.04 This statue, housed in Paris at the Louvre, has been identified as a limestone dog created after the 4th century BCE. As the statue's label indicates: This is not a simple watchdog; this great dog wearing a collar and a bell could be the god Wepwawet, the "opener of the ways" worshipped in Assiout. Wepwawet is often depicted as a wolf standing at the prow of a solar boat. We mostly see him as a bluish or grayish haired wolf to avoid confusion with Anubis, the god associated with mummification and the afterlife in the ancient Egyptian religion, usually depicted as a canine or a man with a canine head. (*Onze Hond* Archive)

A HISTORY OF SHEEPDOGS

Figure 1.05 This metope, a square space between triglyphs in a Doric frieze, shows the Theban hero Actaeon being devoured by Artemis's dogs, and is from a temple at Selinunte, an ancient Greek city on the southwestern coast of Sicily. The head and arms are made of Parian marble and set in limestone. Today, this 5th-century BCE metope is housed in the National Archaeological Museum in Palermo. (*Onze Hond* Archive)

Figure 1.06 In 1926 Louis Huyghebaert wrote about this metope: "The dog repelled by Actaeon's arm looks more like a Malinois than a greyhound. The two dogs that stand closer to the pedestal resemble greyhounds: their bodies and heads are long, and their tails are thin and a bit hairy. There is no question that these two types of dog have been crossed, certainly in the Middle Ages when the two types, especially the hound, occupied such a significant place in relation to humans." (*Onze Hond* Archive)

For a long time now, humans have employed dogs to protect their sheep and goats, and these dogs needed to be big and brave because looting predators were their main enemies. Later, when this protection role became less important, dogs tended toward a smaller stature, and their tasks extended to cattle herding. In England, where the wolf disappeared earlier than in mainland Europe, the shepherd dog made faster progress in his new role, and he soon became smaller than, for example, in Russia, where shepherd dogs are still very big by current standards. When protection became less important, size and sharpness were also less desirable. By the time Stephanitz and certainly Engel were writing, "wolf blood" no longer had a positive connotation. Before then, the opposite was true, when the bigger and more wolf-like your protector dog was, the better.

Sheepdogs

Settlement led people to breed dogs that would be useful guardians. The appearance of these sheepdogs was not important—people cherished their skills and labor performance and selected dogs for breeding based on working qualities.

The task of the dogs, sent out with sheep and goats and shepherds, was to keep the grazers together and protect them against wild animals. Later, they also led cattle to the meadows in the morning and back to the stables in the evening. The size and type of these herding dogs differed from country to country, and even from region to region. Where big, strong, wild animals like wolves and bears lived, cattle were cared for by big, strong dogs.

As the number of big, wild animals in Europe decreased and people broke more ground for agriculture, the need for large protector dogs also decreased and smaller dogs were selected for breeding. As a result, most of the shepherd dogs operating in 18th-century Europe were mid-sized, with thick, rough coats that protected them against all weather conditions. These smaller dogs

A HISTORY OF SHEEPDOGS

Figures 1.07 and 1.08 This 2nd-century BCE mosaic from an atrium at Chebba, Tunisia, is now housed at Tunis's Bardo Museum. In the center, inside a medallion, Neptune, with an aureole around his head, mounts a quadriga towed by four hippocamps. In the corners, within the foliage, four female figures symbolize the seasons. The leashed dog takes his place among the farm workers. (Wikimedia Commons/Jerzystrzelecki)

Figure 1.09 *Enraged Horse* by Paul de Vos (1596–1678), with the landscape painted by Jan Wildens (1586–1653). De Vos and Wildens were Flemish Baroque painters who specialized in compositions of animals, hunting scenes, and still lifes. This painting gives a good view of the different types of dogs one might see in 1630s Belgium. (Wikimedia Commons/State Hermitage Museum, St. Petersburg, Russia)

were agile and lithe, and they also ate less than their larger cousins. In other words, people bred dogs for the purpose and terrains in which they had to work, as well as to stay within the bounds of a slim budget. If a larger dog was not necessary for the work, why pay to feed one? Smaller dogs also did not tire as quickly and could therefore better circle and herd the cattle. They could run fast to an animal that strayed from the herd or into a field to graze. Only those dogs that proved to be excellent workers and adapted to the climate in which they had to do their job were kept and used as breed stock.

Dogs in the Golden Ages

During the 15th and 16th centuries, the Golden Age of Antwerp, and the 17th century, the Dutch Golden Age, Belgian and Dutch societies ushered in the distinction between "noble" and "ignoble" dogs. Hunting dogs in the possession of kings, princes, noblemen, church leaders, and other notables were called noble dogs and were protected by special police laws.

Figure 1.10 A modern Kangal dog in Turkey, wearing a "wolf collar" to protect him from attack, just as Europe's livestock guardian dogs once did. A wolf collar is normally made from iron, and the spikes can be quite long. The collar base protects the dog's throat and carotid arteries, while the spikes help deter bites to the neck and may even injure wolves trying to hurt the dog. (Wikimedia Commons/Abuk Sabuk)

Unprivileged people were forbidden to possess noble dogs, and the countryfolk who kept hunting dogs for their masters were obliged to mark the dogs with the signs of their masters. Lettering or symbols were shaved into the dogs' sides so everyone could see who owned them. By law, these marks had to be maintained and be clear to all. The marked difference between noble and ignoble (in Dutch, *rekel*, in French, *matin*) dogs was also evident in the dissimilarity between the fines levied for stealing one or the other. The thief who stole a noble dog had to pay a fine of six ceurreaalen.[5] Stealing a matin cost the thief only three ceurreaalen! Matins were represented in illustrations of the time as different in type, size, and coat, with many of them outfitted with spiked iron collars, from which we can deduce they protected cattle and farms against wild animals like wolves, which would try to bite the dogs' necks.

During this era, dogs were often named for the professions or businesses of their owners: shepherd dogs, draft dogs, butcher dogs, bleaching-field dogs, and farmer dogs. Matins were not allowed to hunt game and were prevented from doing so by having sticks tied to their necks, which made it impossible for the dogs to chase game through hedges and brushwood without becoming stuck in the undergrowth.

In the 15th century, the city of Antwerp began a phase of rapid development, becoming one of Europe's largest trading cities. In

Figure 1.11 The Antwerp Baroque painter Jacob Jordaens (1593–1678) painted and signed this homely scene in 1638. In the middle is a merry mother surrounded by singing and musical relatives. Even the dog pricks up his ears at the sound of the music—or perhaps he smells the food on the table. Most interesting for our purposes here is that the dog is inside the house, kept as a pet. (Wikimedia Commons/Royal Museum of Fine Arts Antwerp)

1500, the population was 40,000, and by around 1560, 100,000. With increasing prosperity, Antwerp saw unprecedented growth in its population of dogs, and local authorities attempted to control unbridled dog breeding. Drastic local ordinances were promulgated, including the well-known ordinance of 1404, in which the Antwerp magistrate forbade the possession of unspayed bitches and revoked the right to own dogs from those living on charity.

By this time, monasteries, convents, and *beguinages* were also guilty of large-scale production of matins and company dogs. Church councils intervened. The statutes of Antwerp's St. Elizabeth Hospital in 1429, for example, included the following measure:

> In order to stamp out the scandalous abuse the sisters are used to committing with their dogs in the churches, at the tables, and elsewhere, playing with them in less than model ways, we strictly order that no one of them is allowed to keep, feed, or possess dogs, neither their own nor those of other people. If some of them still now have dogs, we order that six days after the issue of this letter they must evict and chase them away, and never possess another one again.

Figure 1.12 Dutch Golden Age painter Adriaen Cornelisz Beeldemaker (1618–1709) specialized in hunting scenes, especially of deer and boar hunts. His paintings were popular, probably because he asked modest prices for them. This painting, *The Hunter* (1653), shows a hunter and his dogs. Doesn't the dog on the left look like a Malinois? (Wikimedia Commons/Rijksmuseum, Amsterdam, the Netherlands)

"STICK MEN"

Sometimes a community was so overrun with dogs that the government had to intervene and send *hondt-slagers* or "stick men" in to chase and catch or simply beat the matins to death. These dog catchers were so loathed by citizens that often only executioners were willing to take on the work. In the city of Antwerp's records from 1584 to 1585, we read: "Paid to Hendrick Van de Berghe, executioner, the sum of forty Artois pounds because he caught 800 dogs at five-cents apiece." In the same order of the Antwerp magistrate, we can read that the hondt-slager was instructed not to beat the "greyhounds, hounds, waterdogs, mastiffs big or small, hunting dogs, or small ones also called lapdogs, and even other dogs who pull the carts, guard the bleaching fields, and ones like them."

Hatred for dog catchers ran so deep that they had to be protected by a law against physical attacks and jeers. In 1657, the Antwerp magistrate published an order that decreed "nobody, whoever he is, is allowed to riot or obstruct the hondt-slager, or throw stones or earth at him, urinate on him, or jeer at him on pain of paying three guilders, besides legal proceedings."

As many dogs were not safe from the hondt-slagers in the streets, they took shelter in churches. The problem became so serious that church councils decided to appoint people to keep the dogs out of the churches. The 1645–1650 accounts of the city of Temsche (near the Schelde River) record that a pension of one Flemish pound and a pair of shoes was granted to the gravedigger because he was responsible for "keeping dogs out of the church." And the ordinance of the city of Leuven (Louvain) from March 28, 1736, reads: "some residents of the city of Louvain are so daring as to come with their dogs into the churches of this city, and by that disturb the peace and quiet in God's temple, the house of prayer." For many years, the door to the entrance hall of Hanswyck Church in Malines carried the words: "Dogs out of God's Temple." When this old admonition was painted is impossible to determine with certainty, but clearly the church guardians were serious about denying shelter to the dogs of Malines.

The Shepherd and His Dogs

An Amsterdam book published in 1640 called *L'agriculture et Maison Rustique* provides a precise description of the matins of that time:

> The shepherd's dog shouldn't be as coarse and big as those of the farm, but as strong and brave ... more long than short, because all animals that are long bodied run faster than those that are short and rectangular. He also should be of white color, so that the shepherd can distinguish him from the wolves, especially in the dark of night.[6]

This shepherd's dog is the forefather of today's Dutch, German, French, and Belgian shepherd dogs.

The same book contains descriptions of the work done by shepherds and their dogs, and their struggles against wolves: "The shepherd taught his dogs to react to certain exclamations

Figure 1.13 Ludovico Guicciardini's 1641 *Description de tous les Pays Bas* (*Description of all the Netherlands*) includes an image of a shepherd's dog. The dog has the appearance of today's Malinois and is portrayed in such a way that the viewer has a sense of his excellent character. The dog's spiked collar leaves us with no doubt about his bite and ability to defending the flock against predators.

and gestures to lead the sheep properly. Furthermore, it is recommended that the shepherd sing or play the flute while the animals are grazing, because the music encourages the sheep to eat well and obey him." The musical shepherd should "preferably have white dogs" and should himself "be clothed in white so as not to frighten the sheep, who seeing other colors are immediately frightened, thinking it might be a wolf come to devour them." The fear of wolves at that time was no small thing, exacerbated by the countless local legends and popular fairy tales in which wolves always played the villains.

To protect his sheep against wolf attacks during the night, the shepherd had to bring his sheep inside a fence and have his dogs walk the fence's perimeter. A 16th-century woodcut, shown here, reveals that wolves on the attack are cunning and coordinated. It is night, and an old wolf is trying to lure the dogs away even as the shepherd comes out of his cart-house to encourage his dogs to chase the old wolf away. Now, the younger wolves have a chance to prey on the sheep.

Figure 1.14 An illustration from master hunter John of Clamorgan's book, *La Chasse au Loup, Nécessaire à la Maison Rustique* (*The Wolf Hunt: Necessary for the Country House*) (c. 1574). This woodcut reveals how intelligent wolves are. At the top right we see an old wolf luring the dogs away, while the younger wolves at the bottom prey on the sheep. (Wikimedia Commons/ Gallica Online Library)

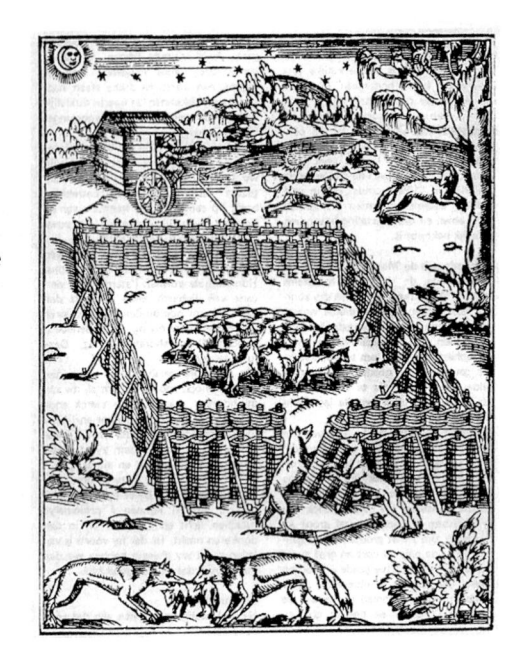

The Poacher's Dog and Other Tasks

Belgian sheepdogs, as well as cattle dogs like the Bouvier des Flandres, almost certainly descend from matins. The smaller and slighter varieties of matin developed in the 18th century by selective breeding with an eye to forming shepherd dogs, as shepherds and farmers didn't need a big, strong dog. This breeding plan also underscores the economic class of people who would be owners of the dogs: poor people who themselves lived and ate frugally. The resulting sheepdogs guarded sheep, cattle, and the farm, and might also pull the cart. Some of these dogs retained a passion for hunting, and so were able companions when the farmers went out to poach game. Given this list of tasks required of them, shepherd dogs had to be lithe, fast, and nimble.

Besides their work as farm helpers and herders, shepherd dogs took on other jobs. Some were effective as aids to night watchmen or soldiers, and some were capable guardians of geese. Breeders of that era

Figure 1.15 A postcard from 1920 of Mr. Jan-Baptist Janssens, the shepherd who had the privilege of grazing his sheep in the royal park of Laeken, with his "mixed Belgian shepherd dogs."

encouraged the best working dogs, selecting dogs for breeding based on their skills, never their exterior characteristics. As a result, there were a wide variety of physical types. The "pure breeding" of the different modern shepherd dogs only started at the end of the 19th century.

In about 1857, in the region of the Belgian towns Oudenaarde, Geeraardsbergen, Ninove, and Edingen, dogs were used as goose guardians. Fifty years later, the geese farms moved toward Lesse and the province Hainaut. Geese farms were also popular in northern France at that time. The dogs helped herd the geese through their life stages in these regions. At the end of June, for example, the young geese were sent in large numbers alongside their dog guardians over public roads to the Belgian geese farms. And at the beginning of December, they were sent to a region near the village of Dendermonde, where they were fattened up. The geese-guarding dogs, most commonly called *ganzenwachters* (goose guards), were sheepdog-like, but their character was considered opposite to that of most sheepdogs, which were then considered "biting" dogs.

Figure 1.16 The Dutch shepherd (Dutch: Hollandse Herdershond) is an Old-World breed of Dutch origin. In times gone by, shepherds and farmers needed a versatile dog adapted to the harsh and sparse existence of the time. The Dutch shepherd dog as we know it today—here, hard at work at his old occupation: herding sheep—evolved from the Dutch shepherd. The modern breed comes in three varieties—long-haired, rough-haired, and short-haired—and is of a medium size (22–24 in / 55–62 cm) and medium weight (51–62 lb / 23–28 kg). The color varies from silver to gold brindle, and in the rough-haired variety blue-gray and salt-and-pepper coloring are allowed. (*Onze Hond* Archive)

During this same era, smugglers found that sheepdogs could help conduct illegal trafficking of goods. They would buckle a special coat around the dogs' bodies, a garment lined with contraband and usually equipped with sharp pins on the outside that made the dogs hard to grab. In Belgium, such dogs were also used for smuggling the famous Brussels lace. In this case, the dogs were first shaved bald before they were wound around with lace. Then, the dogs would be fitted with false coats. The smuggler dogs had to be clever to carry out their duties, which included going through border crossings alone. They were taught to run wide around people in uniform so as not to get caught.

Of course, where one finds smugglers, one also finds customs officers. The latter found that there was only one good weapon against smuggler dogs: customs dogs. By employing dogs, Belgian customs agents could prevent an impressive amount of smuggling. A report from 1907 notes that within six years of work, one customs dog

A HISTORY OF SHEEPDOGS

Figure 1.17 In this 1902 picture from Nord, France, we see two farm boys working with six sturdy dogs and some well-stocked bags of contraband. They are busy loading their dogs with tobacco, coffee, and butter to be transported from France to Belgium. This was a lucrative activity, much safer for the men not to have to carry those bags themselves and risk being shot by the gendarmes. Some dogs did not survive the trip or were taken by the gendarmes, even though all of them were trained (through rough treatment by people in uniforms) to stay away from gendarmes in uniform. (*Onze Hond* Archive)

stopped about 400 smuggler dogs and, in doing so, tracked a large amount of contraband. These dogs were formidable opponents of the smuggler. Pictures from that time of customs officers with their dogs reveal that the heroic animals were, in today's parlance, crossbreeds. Later, customs officers used both Bouviers and Belgian shepherd dogs.

From Interior to Exterior

At the end of the 19th and the start of the 20th century, working farm dogs, like cattle dogs and herding dogs, were bred for many different purposes and tasks; there were no specialists. The farmer or shepherd could not feed more than one dog and needed a multitasker. In the region between the southern provinces of the Netherlands and the northern provinces of Belgium, working dogs who looked like today's Dutch shepherds (Hollandse herders) and Belgian shepherds were often mixed together. Only the best working dog was bred with the best working bitch, regardless of lineage or coat type.

Figure 1.18 As the name indicates, the Bouvier des Flandres (Dutch: Vlaamse Koehond; English: Flanders Cattle Dog) is native to the Belgian and French Flanders regions. The cowmen and drovers of stock in Flanders needed good dogs to drive their herds and so only bred dogs that showed the required physical and behavioral qualities. The dog was also used as a draught or churning dog, but the modernization of farm equipment rendered these tasks obsolete. (*Onze Hond* Archive)

By beginning of the 20th century, however, cynologists had begun the practice of pure breeding, by which the different types of modern dogs originated. A purebred pedigreed dog doesn't just happen; he is the result of the breeder's careful selection of certain traits. At first, the important traits were the working qualities, but as cynologists began determining breed standards, the exteriors of the breeds came into play and in fact somehow became more important than the breeds' individual characters, and so working qualities fell to the wayside of breeding programs. Determining the character of a working dog in the showring is mostly impossible. Many judges were not interested in behavior and character, anyway, but concentrated on rewarding breeders who built beautiful exteriors.

Regardless, the characters and behaviors of cattle dogs (Bouviers and Rottweilers, for example, who independently moved cattle from farmyard to pasture and back again) and shepherd dogs still show clear differences, and are still factors in training these dogs.

The large group of shepherd dogs originally tended flocks of sheep. On the instructions of shepherds, these dogs kept the sheep together and moved them in the determined direction. In the middle of the 19th century, large flocks of sheep were still seen all over Europe, led by shepherds and their dogs. The different varieties within these dogs were similar, except for small regional differences. From these dogs came the modern purebred, pedigreed shepherd dogs.

Individual Choices

Not every dog breed matches every handler, and not every individual dog fits every person. Some affectionate dog breeds, such as those with a strong will to please like the German or Belgian shepherds, normally have a gentle character and bond easily to human caregivers. These sensitive dogs can be easily upset by a poor education. But among these varieties are individual dogs with contrary traits, those who are tough and even obstinate. Still other shepherd dogs have bubbly personalities and are acutely interested in everything that happens in their surroundings. They breathe down their handlers' necks and stay by them all day long. When you send such a dog to his place, he will look aggrieved but will remain attentive to your every move.

Not everyone can work with a sensitive dog, or a tough and obstinate one. And many of us cannot stand to have our dogs hang around at our heels all day. So, you, the handler, must choose carefully which breed to work with. As well, remember that each dog requires certain things from their handlers. If you are a bit short tempered and dominant, it is best not to work with a sensitive dog. You would destroy him in a short time. Quiet people who have the necessary patience can train sensitive dogs to be fast learners and watchful helpers. A stern handler should steer clear of the dogs that stay young at heart for a long time. These dogs mature slowly so need to be treated as puppies for longer. Stern handling early in the game may break these dogs. Remember that sensitivity in dogs does not equal nervousness or shyness. Sensitive dogs are, however, easily ruined when handled in the wrong way.

Most cattle dogs possess a tougher character than shepherd dogs, and they are, in our experience, less inclined to spontaneous cooperate with their handlers. After all, cattle dogs were bred to work independently with large animals. These dogs still retain a very independent character. Training cattle dogs is, in the beginning, a bit more difficult than it is with shepherd dogs, especially when it comes to motivating them to perform certain exercises. They are less amenable, and repeating the same exercises too often may end with these dogs sitting in stubborn silence. It also takes a longer time to teach these dogs to do certain exercises quickly and happily. Nevertheless, we have seen many Bouviers and Rottweilers who are excellent workers. It normally takes more time to bring cattle dogs to the same level as their shepherd dog peers. However, once this level is reached, cattle dogs show that they remember what they're taught better, and often work out the instructions quicker, than the shepherd dogs, even if a cattle dog has not trained for a while.

For example, a Bouvier who didn't work in obedience for about two years was, nevertheless, able to perform his formerly learned exercises very well. This is the opposite of certain shepherd dogs, who, if they have not trained for a long time, are not as able to recall the exercise as quickly and in fact are barely able to work out the instructions, if at all. That said, shepherd dogs are often more willing and diligent in their work. They can also stay in active service longer. Whereas many cattle dogs finish their service at the age of eight years, Malinois can work until 12 years, or even longer. Cattle dogs tend to be heavier and larger than shepherd dogs, and so they age more rapidly and die younger.[7]

2

The Belgian Malinois

Working Sheepdogs

At the end of the 19th century, a variety of working sheepdogs and farm dogs were fulfilling roles all over Europe. They were all rather different from each other in appearance and behavior, depending on the regions in which they were working. In those days, Belgium had many sheepdogs greatly similar in height (50–55 cm / 20–22 in) and weight (about 20 kg / 44 lb), but displaying different coat types. They were all agile and high-spirited dogs, very willing to please the shepherd, but they expressed suspicion and reserve around strangers. Their heads were like those of other sheepdogs in Europe, although their muzzles were not as strong and had pointed snouts. Their small, triangular ears were set high, stiff, and erect, and were often pushed somewhat to the front. They had dark brown, slightly almond-shaped eyes, and their expression indicated alertness, attention, and readiness for action. Their bodies were square with a medium bone structure. These working sheepdogs were accustomed to the rough climate in Belgium, and they were excellent, docile working dogs that went about their work with pleasure.

At this time, cynologists were initially only interested in dogs from other lands, such as the collie and borzoi imported from

Figure 2.01 A shepherd with his sheep on the heath, drawn around 1850 by Simon van den Berg (1822–1891). No day is ever the same for a shepherd and his dog. In spring, the lambs are born, and in the summer, the sheep are shaved. (Wikimedia Commons/Rijksmuseum, Amsterdam, the Netherlands)

England, which at that time were greatly in vogue. There was no interest in domestic farm or herding dogs. However, the work of Professor Adolphe Reul of the Veterinary Highschool of Cureghem (on the outskirts of Brussels) ensured that the domestic Belgian breeds were not forgotten and instead placed in the center of local cynological interest. Together with cynologists Mr. Louis Huyghebaert and Mr. M.L. Van der Snickt, Reul worked to develop the Belgian shepherd dogs into the dog we know today.

Generally, Reul is considered the Nestor of Belgian cynology; no effort was too great for him when it came to stirring up his countrymen's interest in the different varieties of domestic dogs. At the big yearly cattle competition shows, he was the jury member who had to designate the winners. He also represented Belgium at many international meetings. It was his greatest wish to

Figure 2.02 Belgian shepherd dogs drawn in 1899 by Mr. A. Clarys. At the top, Duc, the black long-haired Groenendael owned by Mr. A. Meule; bottom left, Charlois, Mr. J. Verbruggen's short-haired Malinois; and bottom right, Dick, Mr. J. Danelie's wire-haired Laekenois.

retain by inbreeding the outward appearances and characters of the best varieties of domestic sheepdogs. To that end, he wrote a letter to all former students of the Veterinary Highschool of Cureghem to ask these vets to seek out the best and most typical dogs and to ask their owners to bring their animals to a special dog show at the school.

First Meeting, 1891

On November 15, 1891, a total of 117 Belgian shepherd dogs and their owners gathered at the school. Reul wrote in *Les Races de Chiens* (1894):

> How nice they look! No two dogs, even if they were brothers, were look-alikes. I despaired that a typical dog could ever be produced through such a mishmash. Notwithstanding, the problem was tackled by some newly appointed experts, and helped by their imagination, the members of the committee of inquiry reached the decision that probably the Belgian sheepdogs, after being purified of a lot of strange blood, could be divided into three varieties, based on the hair of their coats: long-haired, the wire-haired, and the short-haired...

The coat colors of the dogs were especially different, from black to gray or brown in all shades. The long-haired dogs were mainly black or sometimes brown to dark sable; the short-haired were predominantly brown or beige, mostly with dark masks; and the wire-haired were for the most part gray.

After seriously inspecting and comparing all the dogs, the group founded Club du Chien de Berger Belge in Brussels and decided in the general assembly of April 2, 1892, to accept the official breed standard (in French language and translated into Flemish in 1898), derived from Reul's comparative studies. With this breed standard, Reul indicated his vision of the ideal type, and he advised all the owners of Belgian shepherd dogs only to breed dogs of the same coat variety, without paying attention to the color. By this Reul wanted to establish by inbreeding three types of Belgian shepherd dogs.

First Special Show, 1892

At the first special show organized by the Collie Club and the Club du Chien de Berger Belge, on May 1–2, 1892, in Cureghem (Brussels), 33 short-haired Belgian shepherds were shown: 19 dogs and 14 bitches. The dogs were judged by a Mr. Charles, Reul, and Van der

Figure 2.03 The dogs in this 1910 Clarys sketch are, from left to right, the wire-haired Dick, the short-haired Charlot, and the long-haired Duc—all the desired types of the time. About this drawing, Reul wrote: Mr. Clarys has willingly consented to put his skillful pencil at our service; he reproduced for this work, with rare happiness, the features of the three best models, namely:

Duc, long-haired Belgian shepherd, dark gray brindle, 2.5 years old; winner of first prize at Cureghem, first prize and honorary prize in Brussels, first prize and honorary prize in Antwerp in 1892. Owner: Mr. Arthur Meule, rue de France, in Saint-Gilles.

Charlot, short-haired Belgian shepherd, fawn with black overlay (charbonné) on the back and on the head, white at chest, two years old; first prize Antwerp, second prize Cureghem, second prize Brussels 1892. Owner: Mr. Jean Verbruggen, head of depot at the Brussels Tramways, rue Brogniez.

Dick, wire-haired Belgian sheepdog with gray hair, belonging to Mr. Dagnelie, rue de la Senne, Brussels. This dog is of the same stock as those of the shepherd belonging to Mr. Janssens of Laeken.

Snickt. First prize in the dogs' short-hair class was given to Argus, a fawn dog of Mr. De Bast; second prize went to the strongly black-tinted Charlot of Mr. J. Verbruggen. Charlot was the model for the Malinois sketched by Belgian artist A. Clarys in 1910. Third prize went to Mr. Joseph Auguste's fawn-colored Fox. The prize winners in the bitches' short-haired class, first to third, were Duke (brindle), of Mr. François Wintergroen; Spitz (fawn), of Mr. J.-B. Janssens from Laeken; and Tom (fawn) of Mr. Frans Huyghebaert. (Frans was the brother of cynologist Louis Huyghebaert.) Evidently, in the beginning, coat color was no concern, but that would change later.

Figure 2.04 If you spend a lot of time with one group of animals, you begin to know them as if they were people. This shepherd knew all his sheep, even though the group numbered more than 150. "I knew them all by their faces," he said, adding that this was not unusual. On the contrary, he said, "I know a shepherd who knew his sheep not only by face but also by voice." (*Onze Hond* Archive)

BLACK SHORT-HAIR

All dogs at this first show were also judged on their working capabilities. The competition included several black dogs with short hair, including Paul (a handsome black dog who had only one slight fault and let a single sheep pass). Paul earned fifth place and belonged to Mr. Charles De Mulder, a sheep trader and resident of Vorst. The second prize was awarded to Menneke, a short black dog with short hair, also owned by De Mulder. As Van der Snickt wrote in the Belgian weekly magazine *Chasse et Pêche* (1891), "Menneke is very careful, and he does not make a mistake." If the jury was charged to rely only on a tally of points, Menneke would have won; but "freedom is left to the judges to form their appreciation and render their decision," and the judges estimated Mr. Van Bogget's Milord, from Uccle, superior to the little black dog.

Following Menneke's showing at the 1892 competition, the following text appeared in *Chasse et Pêche* (August 4, 1895):

> We are convinced of the validity of our proposal to adopt a second Belgian sheepdog, which is in any case more Belgian than the first. This dog is small, black, and short-haired. He probably originates from the Schipperke, just as, according to Beckmann, the German sheepdog is derived from the Spits or Keeshond. The dog is highly appreciated as a guard of the herd near Leuven, and is extremely intelligent. He is from the breed that won second prize at the first competition for shepherds on the mainland. He was in Cureghem on May 1 and 2, 1892. According to shepherds and sheep traders, this dog should have won first prize. The judge only awarded him second place because another dog, one that looked like the type of sheepdog that has been proposed as typical, also performed well that day.

In a letter from December 15, 1897, Louis Huyghebaert wrote to Van der Snickt: "I have to report that there is at least one black dog in 20 short-haired sheepdogs. During the cadastral review, I visited all farms from many municipalities in the province, and I have always made the same statement."

By the middle of 1898, the Club du Chien de Berger Belge wanted more homogeneity and so chose a specific color for each type of coat. The revised standard was published in *Chasse et Pêche* on September 24, 1899. There would be only three permitted colors: solid black for the long-haired (Groenendael), dark ash for the wire-haired (Laekenois), and fawn to mahogany (with black tips on the hairs giving an overlay appearance, and preferably a black mask) for the short-haired (Malinois). The rule to reduce to only one color for each variety was strictly applied and has greatly contributed to capturing the fawn with black overlay color in the Malinois.

As a result of this ban on color, the black short-haired type of shepherd dog was not encouraged by breeders. During

Figure 2.05 The black variety of the Malinois is an example of a peculiarity that continues within a breed. It cannot be eradicated. (*Onze Hond* Archive)

Menneke and Paul's time, there were very beautiful types with black, short hair. Anatomically, they had the same structure as the Malinois, except that the hair was generally shorter. Despite ignoring this type in breeding programs after the ban, the black variety is a peculiarity that continues within the breed. It cannot be eradicated, as it is in the genes, and it still exists today in the 21st century.

Figure 2.06 The black Malinois is also often seen as a mixed Malinois, the so-called xMH, which is very often seen in KNPV training in the Netherlands. (*Onze Hond* Archive)

The Club in Malines

In his book *Les Races de Chiens*, published in 1894 in Brussels, Reul writes this about the Malinois:

> Where the short-haired sheepdogs have completely kept their uniformity is in the Antwerp-Kempen region in the direction of the Dutch border, and furthermore in the Dutch province North-Brabant. I was astonished to see, last year, on September 7, 1892, at the show in the Dutch town Oosterhout, some hours' distance from the Belgian border, a dozen sheepdogs of the best-known Belgian short-haired type, belonging to the farmers in the vicinity. I drew a picture of this similar group; they are the size of a fox or wolf, are short-haired and of fawn color; their ears are admirably erect, small, and pointed. Other characteristics: muzzle is moderately pointed, the nose black, the tail well-carried, almost level, but slightly higher to the tip, and hairy, in the shape of an ear of wheat.

Reul's description reveals many characteristics of not only the Malinois but also the short-haired Dutch shepherd dog (in Dutch: *korthaar* Hollandse Herdershond).

At the urgent request of Reul, in 1898 in Malines (in Flemish: Mechelen), Louis Huyghebaert and some Malinois enthusiasts such as veterinarian Dr. Gustaaf Geudens, founded the Mechelse Club tot Verbetering van den kortharigen Schaapshond (Malinois Club to Improve the Short-Haired Sheepdog). This club was a branch of the Club du Chien de Berger Belge, the main club in Brussels. Its aim was to improve the type of the short-haired Belgian shepherd dog, especially the one bred near Malines, the city from which the name of the variety is derived. In the same year this Malines club published an illustrated pamphlet in which for the first time the official breed standard was translated into Flemish.

Color and Hair Varieties

In the beginning, Belgian shepherds were classified as either long-, wire-, or short-haired without distinction of color. Viewed in the light of that era's keen interest in foreign dogs, it is understandable that during the first five years of the breed's rebirth, the Belgian shepherd wasn't taken seriously. The Société Royale St. Hubert (in Dutch: Koninklijke Maatschappij St. Hubertus [KMSH]), since 1911 the official kennel club of Belgium for the Fédération Cynologique Internationale (FCI), did not record the Belgian shepherd dog in its stud book. "It was only after a degrading 'traineeship' of a decade that he, in terms of being recorded in the stud book, at last was placed on the same level as that strange, but long-recognized Scottish shepherd dog, the aristocratic collie," Louis Huyghebaert wrote in 1899. But before the Belgian shepherd dog was admitted to this "knighthood," the breed first had to take on a distinct appearance, which on Reul's advice was obtained by inbreeding and selection. It would not be until 1900 that the first two varieties of Belgian shepherds, the Malinois and the Groenendael, were recorded in the stud book, the *Livres des Origines St. Hubert* (*LOSH*), of the Société Royale St. Hubert–KMSH.

But it took even more time before all could agree about the colors and hair varieties of Belgium's typical, native shepherd dogs. During the following years, the prime movers among the Belgian shepherd enthusiast community set to work with great determination to unify the type and correct the faults. Soon after, the desired type and temperament of the Belgian shepherd was established. During the history of the Belgian shepherd, the issue of differing but acceptable varieties and colors led to many heated discussions. Any issue involving the breed's morphology, temperament, and suitability for work, however, has never caused any disagreement.

In 1899 the Club du Chien de Berger Belge, in agreement with the KMSH, suggested specific coat colors for each of the three hair types. This decision was one-sided, set down by the main club in Brussels without consulting the club in Malines. The determination was as follows: black for the long-haired, ash gray for the wire-haired, and fawn with black tips on the hairs (fauve charbonné) and a black mask for the short-haired. This ruling was described by Louis Huyghebaert in "Onze Belgische Rashonden" (1926) as "a sort of revolt" that had negative consequences for the future breeding of the Belgian shepherd. The Brussels club made the decision because they wished to follow the same track the English took when promoting their collie to the world. First, the collie was "elected" by inbreeding, and thereafter breeders chose pairs based on phenotype, without interest in training or work abilities.

Figure 2.07 Alex Van Kerckhove from Malines in Belgium made these beautiful drawings, nicely depicting, especially, the tracking Malinois and his brother, lying down, closely listening for his master's call. Together with the third standing dog, these sketches do a fine job of representing the breed in the early 20th century. (*Onze Hond* Archive)

A Working Dog

The shepherd enthusiasts in Malines had another perspective: above all, their shepherd dog had to be a working dog. In their view, appearance alone did not qualify a dog for breeding, but the combination of exterior and interior was vital to the establishment of the breed. They preferred well-trained dogs that were also well-built and, according to Huyghebaert's "Onze Belgische Rashonden," had a "sound and smart appearance." The coat color was only a matter of minor importance. They were afraid the Malinois would become a "fancy" dog, that his terrific character would be lost. For these reasons, Louis Huyghebaert asserted the necessity of organizing matches for trained guard and defense dogs. Nowhere in Belgium (or elsewhere) had such working competitions ever taken place. He organized meetings with Reul and Van der Snickt, and then they contacted the police superintendent of Ghent, Mr. Van Wesemael. They visited demonstrations of the dog's ability, and again and again the Malinois showed excellent working-dog characteristics.

The first public working competition was 1903 in Malines, organized by the Malinois Club. The first prize winner was Cora I, a bitch with a white spot on her breast, owned by Mr. L. Opdebeeck, a bleacher from Malines. Cora I, together with other famous dogs of that time, would lay the foundation for today's Malinois. But the breed hadn't reached that stage yet.

The controversy about the Belgian decision regarding coat colors hadn't faded. At the working competitions, among the prize-winning short-haired dogs were found very pale-colored types. However, the decision about coat colors closed the door on dog shows for all those Belgian shepherds who did not fit into the new categories. To avoid a quarrel between members of the same club, albeit different branches, the breeders from Malines finally accepted the decision, and from 1903 on, the Malinois breed included only "fawn" dogs "with black mask and overlay."

Famous Dogs from the Breed's Early Years

For a clear picture of the famous dogs from this period, the early 1900s, we must first look at the shepherd Mr. J.-B. Janssens, who had the privilege of grazing his sheep in the royal park of Laeken. His best dogs were pale, fawn-colored, wire-haired Belgian shepherds (Laekenois), but Janssens wasn't worried about his dogs' coats, and when breeding them, he crossed all coat varieties. According to Reul, his motto was: "A good dog can't wear a bad suit." One of his dogs was the wire-haired Vos de Laeken, sometimes

Figure 2.08 The ancestors of the Malinois and the Laekenois, Vos (Dutch word for "fox") and Liske were owned by the shepherd Janssens of Laeken who was allowed to graze his flock of sheep in the public gardens of the royal palace in Laeken, near Brussels. In 1892 Vos (also called Vos I) won third prize at the last sheep dog test organized by the Club du Chien de Berger Belge. (Last, because the event was not financially viable.) Vos was a yellow, rough-haired dog and became the ancestor of the wire-haired (Laekenois) variety.

also called Vos II. Reul wrote this about the dog in *Chasse et Pêche* (October 2, 1896):

> I gave the first prize to Vos II of Mr. Janssens, an exceptional breeder of wire-haired shepherds. I confess, however, that I was lenient, so I could encourage a professional shepherd. Anyway, Vos II is a working dog and no fancy shepherd dog. One can daily see him working near the flock in the royal park of Laeken. For sure, Vos isn't a bad model, but his flaxen-colored coat is too long for a "wire-haired" dog, too long especially at his tail, which also itself is too long. It is almost a bushy tail. This doesn't give me much satisfaction. Verily, Mr. Janssens has bred better dogs.

Shepherd Janssens also owned the gray-brindle short-haired bitch Liske de Laeken. From a cross of the yellowish wire-haired Vos de Laeken (also called Vos I) and Liske de Laeken, he bred,

Origin of the Malinois

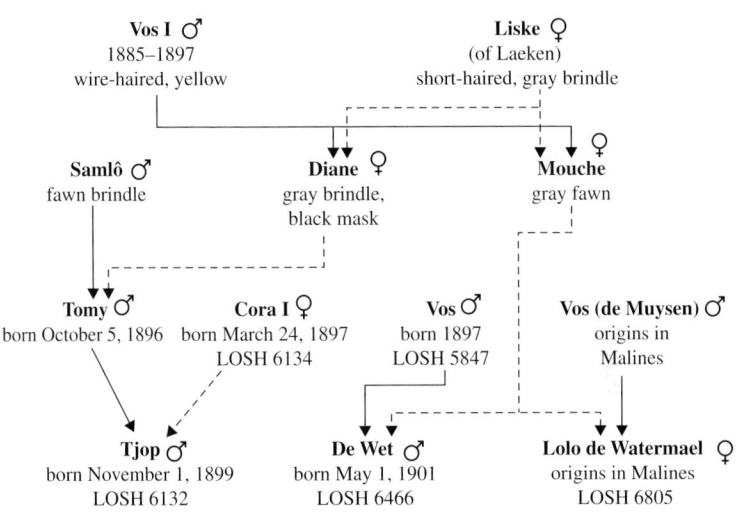

```
Vos I ♂                                    Liske ♀
1885–1897                                  (of Laeken)
wire-haired, yellow                        short-haired, gray brindle

        Samlô ♂           Diane ♀                    Mouche ♀
        fawn brindle      gray brindle,              gray fawn
                          black mask

   Tomy ♂          Cora I ♀          Vos ♂          Vos (de Muysen) ♂
born October 5, 1896  born March 24, 1897  born 1897       origins in
                      LOSH 6134        LOSH 5847           Malines

        Tjop ♂              De Wet ♂              Lolo de Watermael ♀
 born November 1, 1899   born May 1, 1901        origins in Malines
     LOSH 6132              LOSH 6466                LOSH 6805
```

Figure 2.09 Origin of the Malinois.

among others, the bitches Diane and Mouche. Mouche's coat color was gray-fawn brindle. Diane was a fierce animal, pale-gray brindle with black mask and small, erectly carried ears. Her coat was somewhat wiry.

Diane was bred to a very typical short-haired shepherd dog, pale brindle with a handsome exterior, called Samlô, owned by P. Beernaert from Brussels, and from that combination came the dog Tomy, sometimes called the ancestor of the short-haired variety. His coat color met all the requirements of the Brussels coat decision. Owned by Mr. Segers in Brussels, Tomy was a beautiful dog with a rich fawn color and black mask. When the breeders from Malines and vicinity saw this dog, they were enthusiastic. It didn't take long before all the bitches were mated with him. One of those was Opdebeeck's Cora I, the winner of the first working competition. The parents of Cora I are unknown—at the time, no one kept a stud book—but we do know that she descended from very good working dogs from Malines.

Figure 2.10 The typical short-haired pale-brindle shepherd dog Samlô, owned by Mr. P. Beernaert from Brussels, was a dog with a handsome exterior. Samlô and Diane—a fierce, pale-gray brindle bitch with a black mask, who had a somewhat wiry coat—together produced the dog Tomy.

Figure 2.11 Samlô and Diane's Tomy was owned by Mr. H. Segers from Brussels. Tomy is sometimes called the ancestor of the short-haired variety of Belgian shepherds.

TJOP AND DE WET

From Tomy and Cora I came the dog Tjop, who was registered in the *LOSH*, KMSH's official stud book, under the number LOSH 6132. Tjop had a fine appearance and desirable working-dog characteristics. Another famous dog of the time, De Wet (LOSH 6466), owned by the brothers Mairesse in Frameries, became Tjop's chief competitor for a time.

De Wet descended from Mouche, Mrs. Duchenoy's gray-fawn bitch, who came from Vos de Laeken and Liske de Laeken. De Wet's sire was another Vos (LOSH 5847), a dog of unknown origin, who descended from the fine working dogs of Malines, and was owned by Miss Vanhaesendonck from Antwerp. This Vos won, among other awards, first prize at the dog show in Mons in 1899. Dr. V. Fally, a judge at the 1903 specialty show in Brussels, described Vos in *Chasse et Pêche* thus: "Head is too short, and the hairs have no black overlay."

Sixty-nine short-haired Belgian shepherds entered this 1903 show, and Fally further wrote: "I don't think there have ever been

Figure 2.12 The breeders from Malines sought talented dogs who were well-built, intelligent, and friendly. In 1903 a large exhibition for shepherd dogs was organized in the botanical garden of Malines, followed by a large work test, which also involved water work. The first prize was won by Cora I, owned by Mr. L. Opdebeeck from Malines. Bred with Tomy, she became the mother of the famous dog Tjop.

Figure 2.13 Frans Huyghebaert, brother of writer and judge Louis Huyghebaert, was the owner of Tjop (LOSH 6132), one of the most important Malinois of the era. Tjop was born on November 1, 1899. His father Tomy was an exceptional guard dog, and his mother Cora I was the first-place winner in the 1903 exhibition. Tjop had an excellent appearance, perfect bone structure and angles, and good color (even without a mask), and he was a very good working dog, despite being extremely nervous. He was 22 inches (57 cm) tall at the shoulders, his back was a little long, the legs a little too fine, and he had some rough hair on the croup.

Figure 2.14 Tjop fully deserves the honor of the bronze relief made by Mr. Tuerlinckx. With his opponent De Wet, Tjop represents one of the two pillars of the Malinois breed.

Figure 2.15 De Wet, owned by the brothers Mairesse in Frameries, had Vos (also called Vos de Polders) for a father and the gray-fawn Mouche for a mother. At the dog show in Brussels in 1902, De Wet was described as follows: "60 cm [24 in] tall, a remarkable dog, well-built with an excellent coat, remarkably good shoulders and chest. Good topline and croup, good head, flawless tail carriage, small triangular ears, excellent overall appearance. Only the color is somewhat pale. This error is compensated by the very good mask and the shoulders."

better dogs united. It is always the club from Malines that beats everything, which doesn't surprise, since the Malines area is recognized as the home of this variety of the Belgian shepherd dog. The breed is by selection more or less established, the obtained products are more typical, and, generally speaking, there is more uniformity in the different show classes."

Unlike Vos, Vos's progeny, De Wet, kicked up a lot of dust. Judge Esq. Henri Van Albada de Haan Hettema described him at the 1902 Brussels dog show, again in *Chasse et Pêche*, as:

> a beautiful dog; a good walker, with excellent hair structure (recommended highly); nervous, with a lot of expression; excellent in shoulders, body, loin, and the backhand; a good head (that gives satisfaction); perfect tail carriage; small ears of good triangle shape. Generally speaking, excellent. But, because nothing is perfect, the color is a bit too pale. This fault, however, is nullified by the mask and the shoulders that are strongly colored. De Wet surpasses his competitors from the view of a complete build.

Tjop was De Wet's competitor at this show, and Van Albada described him, as well. "Tjop, often described by qualified experts,

Figure 2.16 In 1902 Judge Esq. Van Albada had excellent things to say about Tjop, but he also wrote that he was "too slim." This pronouncement agitated many people in Malines—after all, if Tjop was too slim, then breeders should breed their dogs heavier, but that was against the breed standard.

Figure 2.17 Tjop's clean-cut and well-carried head lacked the black mask.

is also excellent, spirited, and smart. Nevertheless, he shows too slim for a stud dog. While De Wet is too pale colored, despite his black overlay, Tjop is rich in color, although he misses the overlay." These pronouncements created a lot of agitation, especially in the Malines region, because discrimination against Tjop based on his being "too slim," could mean that breeders were being encouraged to breed their dogs heavier, and that was against the breed standard.

However, at the special exhibition for shepherd dogs in Brussels on April 19, 1903, Dr. Fally judged the dogs and gave Tjop first prize in the open class, writing in *Chasse et Pêche*: "Tjop, well-known winner, presents masterly, splendid in build, strong, clean-cut, and well-carried head, good color, has no black mask, tail a bit too highly carried."

At the same show, De Wet was awarded second, earning this judgment from Fally: "Comes near to the previous, well-built, although the breast is a bit too broad, and the same for the head. The cheeks are too ponderous; the coat is flaxen colored."

And one year later in Brussels, Judge Reumon named Tjop the champion, reporting in *Chasse et Pêche*: "Tjop is a dog of the ideal type. He combines strength and elegance; power of reason and resolution radiate from his eyes. The movement is proud and noble; his attitude is that of a thoroughbred animal." In contrast, by 1904, De Wet had completely disappeared from places of honor at shows, and Dr. Fally refused to give him a prize in the open class, in which he qualified Tjop as the best dog.

Development of the Malinois

De Wet and Tjop, and the various judgments about their appearance and qualities, took an active part in the development of the Malinois, as the breed was called after 1900. Via their bloodlines—and branches bearing the likes of Lolo de Watermael, a half-sister of De Wet from Vos de Muysen of Mr. Van Camp—the Malinois we know today took shape.

A famous relative of Tjop and De Wet was Ninon de l'Enclus, owned by Edgard Couvreur of Amougies, a well-known breeder from the Belgian province Hainault. Ninon was so perfect that from 1907 to 1914, she continually gained first place at dog shows. Another famous Malinois from the period before World War I was Fram du Bois de la Deule (LOSH 8297), French Champion, owned by Mr. Danna from Lille in the northern part of France. Both famous and lesser-known Malinois of that time trace their pedigrees back to Tjop and De Wet.

In his article, "Onze Belgische Rashonden," printed in the Belgian magazine *Cultura* (1926), Louis Huyghebaert wrote about that period: "Meanwhile, several breeders have driven the family breeding on Tjop further." In particular, he mentioned Mr. Marcel Cotte's kennel Elfes, which had obtained a first-class breeding animal in Rolf des Elfes (Tjop's grandson). And Mr. Ridder Hynderick de Theulegoet's kennel, Ter Heide, at the time preferred a stud dog named Knap ter Heide, a son, grandson, and great-grandson of Tjop.[8] Huyghebaert continued, "These two kennels, and others, disappeared during the 1914–1918 war years and under the post-war dogs, none of Tjop's direct descendants have come up as 'big' dogs."

Before World War I, many Malinois were bred in the Malines area, especially after the price campaigns for police dogs—see chapter 5, The Malinois as Police Dog—had publicly announced the good reputation of the Malinois. By chance, one of these Malines-area dogs, Wip (bred by Mr. Beullens from Sint-Katelijne-Waver), came into very good hands. Tjop was Wip's father, and his mother was a daughter of Tjop. Although not without faults, Wip was noticeable for the noble lines of his head and his typical expression. He was sold to a Frenchman from the neighborhood of Valenciennes, and after he was seen there by a Malinois expert from Bergen, he was returned to Belgium. In the region Frameries, Wip found in the bitches descending from De Wet very suitable breeding material. He gave the best offspring to daughters of Tjop, such as Beth, who produced Tititte and Dingo with Wip.

Dingo (LOSH 8199) joined a leading breeder, Mr. Dupuis from Braquegnies in the province Hainaut. Although Dingo was

THE BELGIAN MALINOIS

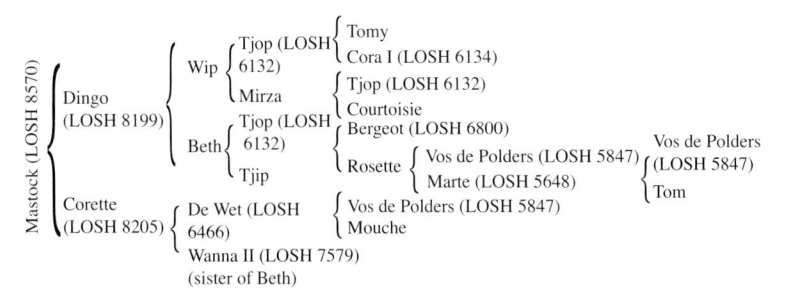

Mastock (LOSH 8570) {
  Dingo (LOSH 8199) {
    Wip {
      Tjop (LOSH 6132) { Tomy / Cora I (LOSH 6134)
      Mirza
    Beth {
      Tjop (LOSH 6132) { Tjop (LOSH 6132) / Courtoisie
      Tjip { Bergeot (LOSH 6800) / Rosette { Vos de Polders (LOSH 5847) { Vos de Polders (LOSH 5847) / Tom } / Marte (LOSH 5648) }
  Corette (LOSH 8205) {
    De Wet (LOSH 6466) { Vos de Polders (LOSH 5847) / Mouche
    Wanna II (LOSH 7579) (sister of Beth)
}

Figure 2.18 Mastock's pedigree.

only available for breeding for a short time, he still helped produce some stars like the previously mentioned Fram du Bois de la Deule and Mastock (See Mastock's pedigree, Figure 2.18). Mastock's dame was Corette, a daughter of De Wet and Wanna II, a sister of the aforementioned Beth, and thus Tjop's daughter.

The ancestor of Mr. Danna's kennel was Flèche II, a daughter of Tjop and Lolo de Watermael. By mating her with Duc de Bruges, Mr. Danna obtained Javotte du Bois de la Deule, who, with the beautiful lion's color of the father and a mild black mask, unfortunately sometimes produced offspring with floppy ears.

The same crossing of De Wet with bitches descending from Tjop produced excellent dogs. From Beth, for example: Djecko des Bas Jardins, Rip des Trieux, and Cabaret. Beth's sister, Wanna II, mated with De Wet to produce a beautiful bitch, Corette, from whom many beautiful scions came. Her best son was Mastock.

Before World War I, Rip (son of De Wet) and Cora produced Toreador. He often competed with Fram du Bois de la Deule in the show ring and from his line came one of the best bitches of that time: Sahra de la Dendre, who lived in France. Her family tree (see Sahra de la Dendre's pedigree, Figure 2.19) gives a striking example of the intersections in Tjop's and De Wet's bloodlines.

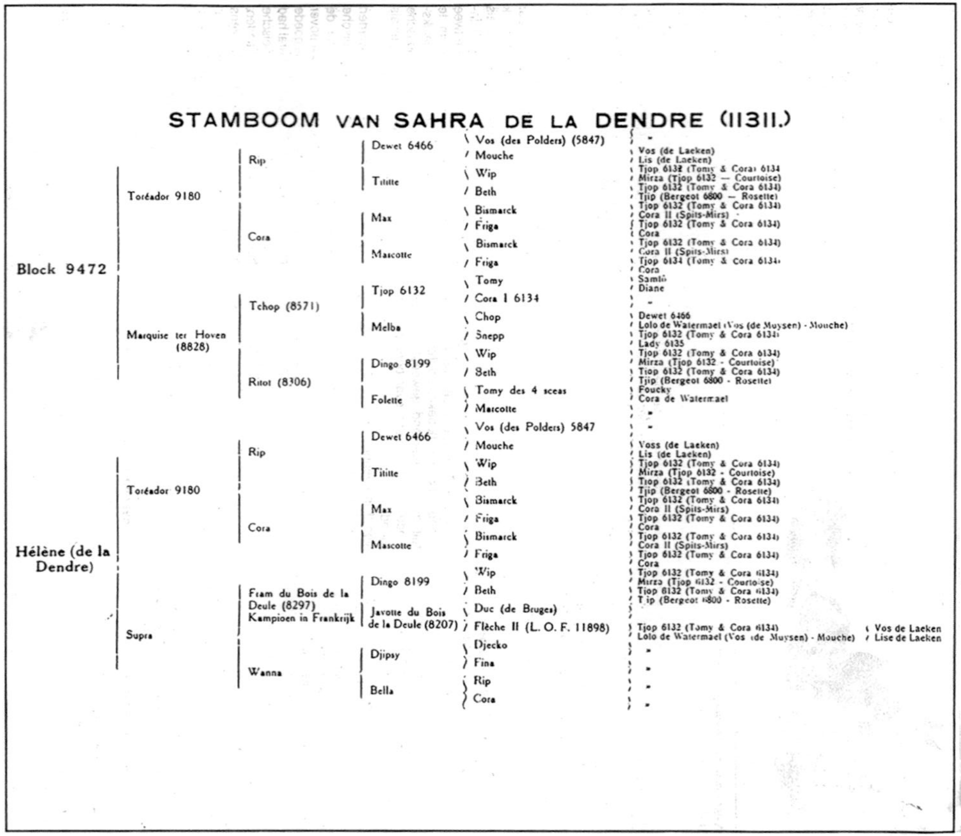

Figure 2.19 Sahra de la Dendre's family tree reveals the connections between Tjop's and De Wet's bloodlines.

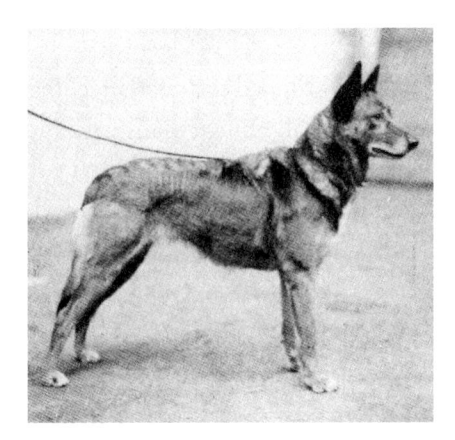

Figure 2.20 Ninon de l'Enclus (LOSH 8209), bred and owned by Edgard Couvreur of Amougies, had De Wet (LOSH 6466) for a sire and Cora de l'Enclus—a daughter of Tjop (LOSH 6132)—for a mother. Ninon was an unbeatable bitch in her glorious time, but the rest of her littermates were rather average. She won 72 first prizes, 69 prizes of honor, 74 special prizes, and 34 CACs (Certificat d'Aptitude au Championnat, the national championship prize) before World War I. When used as a brood bitch after her show career, Ninon was bred to Tjop (her maternal grandfather), and gave birth to the CAC winner Forban de l'Enclus.

Mastock found in Bella (whose sire was Cabaret) the ideal bitch to produce typical Malinois. The many good dogs descended from them include: Tjippo, Khaki, Sady-Lancier, Fabrice, and Zède.

Three other stud dogs also began to draw attention: Tomy, Loupo, and Vainqueur. In 1921 Tomy and Dianelle, a daughter of Tjippo, produced an excellent litter, of which the best was Pélo du Bois de la Deule. Despite his slight figure, Pélo was so typical to what Malinois breeders wanted that he drew first place, over and over. Loupo was a beautiful, heavy dog who also contributed to some excellent litters, but at the age of three he was found dead in his kennel. Vainqueur, true to his name, as Louis Huyghebaert wrote in 1926, "conquered all opponents in the ring."

By 1907, the first Malinois had been exported to other countries. From that period until World War II, many Malinois were shipped to dog enthusiasts in the United States.

After World War I

World War I (1914–1918) temporarily stopped the good breeding of Malinois. The disruption of war not only ruined many valuable breeding animals but also the breeding program that had been going on for many years. To broaden the breeding base after the war, breeders were at first forced to pay little attention to coat color in favor of maintaining and even improving correct character. So, once again, the Malinois appeared a variety of colors. Especially near Malines, after a brief time, the short-haired type thrived.

Figure 2.21 This perfectly homogenous, typical group of Malinois owned by Mr. Georges Danna from Lille, France, created a sensation at the shows, rewarding a judiciously conducted breeding program that combined Tjop's elegance and color with De Wet's strength and structure. On the left sits Fram du Bois de la Deule, who was in 1913 French Champion of Beauty. This was when the kennel was at its peak. The birth of many other champions was anticipated, but in 1914, war unfurled in Belgium and northern France, destroying everything in its path and ruining the results of 10 years of patient work on the breed.

THE BELGIAN MALINOIS

Figure 2.22 René Delin made this portrait in 1921 of the three most desired head types of the period. From right to left: the long-haired Tervueren, the short-haired Malinois, and the wire-haired Laekenois.

Post-war breeders continued to give attention to the dog's working abilities and training.

In the period between the two world wars, many long-haired Malinois appeared. The most important among them are the descendants of the long-haired fawn Tervueren Minox (LOSH 15141), born May 6, 1921, son of Malinois Minox (LOSH 10043) and Nina (see the pedigree for Minox, Figure 2.23). Minox was born in Arthur Hanappe's kennel, De Jolimont, which blazed a trail for interwar Malinois breeders, producing a great many beautiful working dogs.

During this era, Mr. Felix Verbanck established his famous and flourishing Malinois kennel, De l'Ecaillon, after acquiring the celebrated Sibelle de Jolimont from Hanappe. He bred Sibelle with some proven studs from Mr. A. Crunelle's Pimprenelles kennel, as well as to some consanguine studs. In this way, he endowed De l'Ecaillon with some beautiful Malinois: Fram and Fidele,

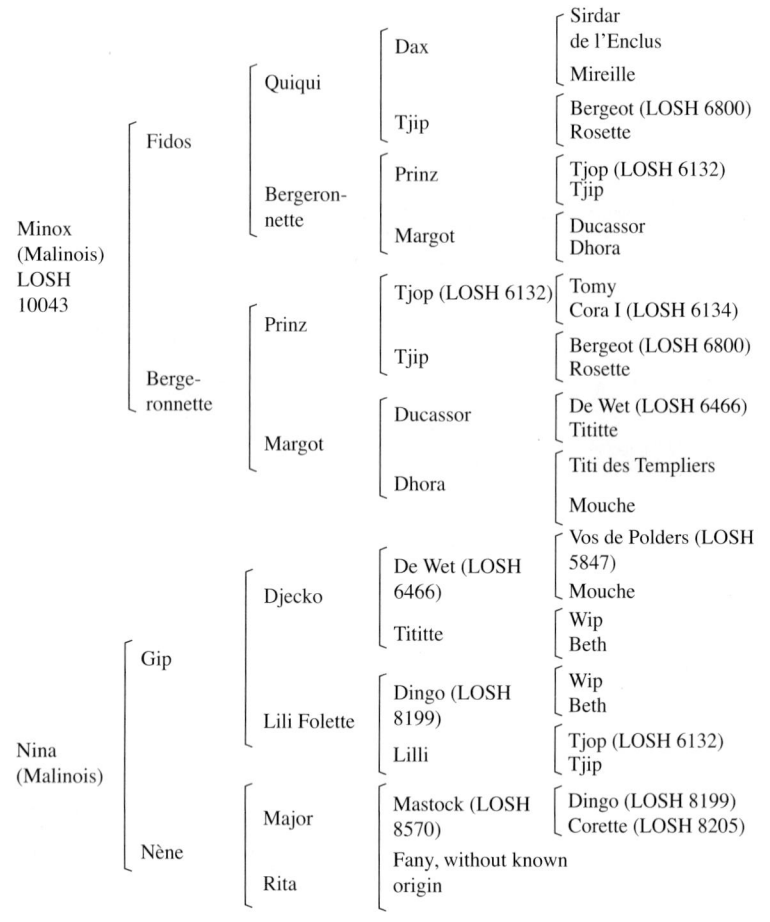

```
                                                    ┌─ Sirdar
                                        ┌─ Dax ─────┤  de l'Enclus
                                        │           └─ Mireille
                           ┌─ Quiqui ───┤
                           │            │           ┌─ Bergeot (LOSH 6800)
                           │            └─ Tjip ────┤
                           │                        └─ Rosette
             ┌─ Fidos ─────┤
             │             │            ┌─ Prinz ───┬─ Tjop (LOSH 6132)
             │             │            │           └─ Tjip
             │             ├─ Bergeron- ┤
             │             │  nette     │           ┌─ Ducassor
Minox        │             │            └─ Margot ──┤
(Malinois)   │                                      └─ Dhora
LOSH      ───┤
10043        │                          ┌─ Tjop ────┬─ Tomy
             │                          │  (LOSH    └─ Cora I (LOSH 6134)
             │             ┌─ Prinz ────┤  6132)
             │             │            │           ┌─ Bergeot (LOSH 6800)
             │             │            └─ Tjip ────┤
             └─ Berge- ────┤                        └─ Rosette
                ronnette   │                        ┌─ De Wet (LOSH 6466)
                           │            ┌─ Ducassor ┤
                           │            │           └─ Tititte
                           └─ Margot ───┤
                                        │           ┌─ Titi des Templiers
                                        └─ Dhora ───┤
                                                    └─ Mouche

                                        ┌─ De Wet ──┬─ Vos de Polders (LOSH
                                        │  (LOSH    │  5847)
                           ┌─ Djecko ───┤  6466)    └─ Mouche
                           │            │           ┌─ Wip
                           │            └─ Tititte ─┤
             ┌─ Gip ───────┤                        └─ Beth
             │             │            ┌─ Dingo ───┬─ Wip
             │             │            │  (LOSH    └─ Beth
             │             └─ Lili ─────┤  8199)
             │                Folette   │           ┌─ Tjop (LOSH 6132)
Nina      ───┤                          └─ Lilli ───┤
(Malinois)   │                                      └─ Tjip
             │                          ┌─ Mastock  ┌─ Dingo (LOSH 8199)
             │             ┌─ Major ────┤  (LOSH ───┤
             │             │            │  8570)    └─ Corette (LOSH 8205)
             └─ Nène ──────┤            └─
                           │            ┌─ Fany, without known
                           └─ Rita ─────┤  origin
```

Figure 2.23 Pedigree of the long-haired fawn Tervueren Minox (LOSH 15141), born May 6, 1921, son of the Malinois Minox (LOSH 10043) and the Malinois Nina. Minox (LOSH 15141) came from De Joliment, a kennel that produced excellent working dogs during the interwar period.

Gladiateur and Glaneur, Ivan and Ideal—all highly praised champions of the time.

Other important interwar kennels were De Hallattes and Du Forgeron, with the champions Abella and Benny; and De Grand Rabot, with the champions César and Ecapi.

Champions and competitors would have taken part in two interesting dog events that took place after World War I in

Belgium: a training contest for police dogs in Antwerp on July 3, 1921, organized by the Antwerp club, De Afgerichte Hond (The Trained Dog); and an exhibition for shepherd dogs and cattle drivers put together by Canine Société de Malines on July 10 of the same year. At the time, especially in the area around Malines, Belgians showed great interest in dog training. Many enthusiasts focused attention on the work of national police dog breeds (Malinois, Groenendael, Dutch shepherd, and German shepherd). In Belgium and in the Netherlands and France, people showed interest in other competitions, such as those related to obedience and security (jumping, guarding, attacks, defending handlers, and so on). However, most Malines and Antwerp trainers taught their dogs exercises that prepared the dogs for practical service. Thus, competitions took on the same theme.

In 1921, the magazine *De Nederlandsche Hondensport* (*The Dutch Dog Sport*) reported:

> The test in Antwerp was held partly on land adjacent to the docks, between piles of wood. The obedience and jumping exercises, for which many natural obstacles were chosen, generally didn't pose problems, but when it came to exercises outside the program of regular training, the dogs' performance levels declined. When searching for the decoy between the piles of wood, almost all dogs searched throughout the site, but all except one didn't understand what they were looking for. They would walk over to the decoy, who had concealed himself in a corner, pass by him, and then later return to the same place and see him there, but would still not take notice of him.
>
> For the next exercise, an ambush was staged. Within sight of the dog, but at a distance, some people shouting loudly and making wild gestures stood, fired some shots, and then walked away. Then the dog handler was unexpectedly attacked by a hidden decoy. None of the competing dogs seemed to care about their bosses after having seen the spectacle of the people

shooting guns, even though all the dogs had fine character and aptitude. Their response was the inevitable consequence of unilateral bite training.

The prizes were awarded as follows: first prize, Rita de la Campine, the Malinois bitch of Mr. Bogemans from Antwerp; second prize, Duc du Rupel, the Malinois dog of Mr. Vonkanel from Antwerp; third prize, Snap [Fram de Jolimont], the Malinois dog from Mr. H. Hanssen from Antwerp; fourth prize, Tom, a Briard dog of Mr. Crombrugge from Boom.

These four prize winners also participated in a water working competition, consisting of on-command jumping into the water, retrieving a floating object out of the water, and rescue of a "drowning" doll. All dogs showed good work, with the result that Duc du Rupel came in first, Rita de la Campine second, Tom third, and Snap [Fram de Jolimont] fourth.

The 1921 exhibition at Malines had 80 dogs participating: 33 Malinois; 13 Groenendaels (1 rough haired, 2 short haired); 1 Tervueren; 10 Bouviers des Flandres; 1 Bouvier d'Ardennes; 15 German shepherd dogs; and 4 matins.

The number of Malinois present show that there are sufficient good representatives of this breed available. But they are not exhibited as much as, especially the Groenendaels. At foreign exhibitions, the numbers of breeds present are usually just the opposite. But it is a pity that abroad, in the Netherlands, as well as everywhere else, the introduction of the Malinois to the show ring has so far been ignored by exhibitors and breeders. He should earn at least as much interest and appreciation as the Groenendael, considered the universal representative of Belgian sheepdog, breeding beyond the borders of his native country. According to the opinion of most trainers, however, the character and aptitude for training of the Malinois is highly preferred to that of the Groenendael.

The magazine also mentioned Block and Césary as champions, with Block as the winner at the 1921 Malines exhibition.

Block is undoubtedly the best in construction, but is beginning to show the traces of his age, while apparently age does not touch seven-year-old Césary. Among the other dogs, Tarsam, Khaki [see Khaki's pedigree, Figure 2.24], and Raky (all three by Mastock from Bella,) are the best.

Mr. de Laveleye's Marpha's beautiful head helped her gain first prize in the winners' class bitches, and in the championship battle, she was victorious over Héléna de la Dendre (the award winner of the open class), who had qualities and faults similar to Marpha . . . . [the best color, however] is Bobinnette. And in Marcella we see a bitch of the old type, with lots of chest and substance, also a good head and beautiful expression. In standing position, she shows excellently, both in forehand and behind, but when moving, nine-year-old Marcella shows her age, especially in the hindquarters.

Fram de Jolimont was born August 10, 1917, in the Jolimont kennel. Renamed Snap and trained by Mr. Henri Hanssen of Antwerp, Snap grew into the unquestionable star of all the trials at this time. This was, of course, a great propaganda for the Malinois among the training enthusiasts back then. Mr. Hanssen trained this intelligent dog well, even though at first, he was quite an aggressive and biting character. He inherited his

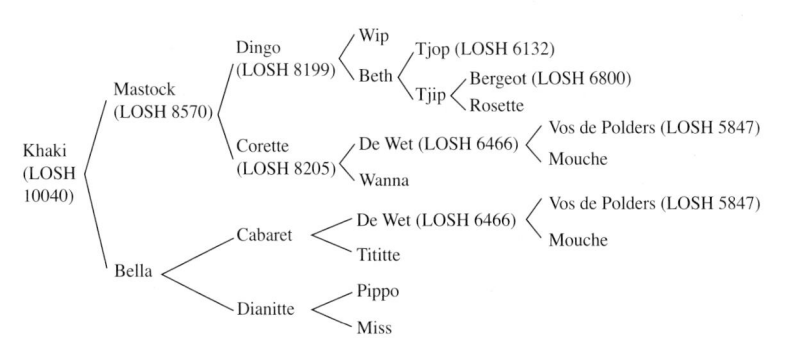

Figure 2.24 Khaki's pedigree.

Figure 2.25 Snap (LOSH 10050) was born Fram de Jolimont on August 10, 1917, son of sire Fidos (de Jolimont) and dam Picpus (Arthur Hanappe). He was an ace in ringsport, defending and guarding, and field work, including water work and tracking. In 1925 he became a working champion. He also was an important exhibition and stud dog. He was the father of many famous working Malinois: Sam du Thiriau, second at the 1926 Grand Prix of Belgium; Killer, who worked in 1924; and daughter Mascotte du Tigre Royal, who was tracking champion in 1928.

aggressive temperament from his grandfather on father's side, Sips ter Heide (son of Tjop and Zet [LOSH 8210]), who came from the Ter Heide kennel of Louis Huyghebaert (who did not like biting dogs). Snap became a champion in 1925 by achieving different national beauty awards as well as prizes in tracking and other working matches. He stands with his sons and daughters at the origin of the main bloodlines of the Malinois working dogs. As *The Dutch Dog Sport* reported, "Snap has a stubborn and wild character. From the moment his master is attacked, he defends him with fire."

Belgian Ringsport

In 1926 KMSH organized the national "ringsport" competition for the first time under the name Grand Prix of Belgium. That year, the Malinois bitch Sadi (LOSH 13537), won the contest. Second was the dog Samox (LOSH 20606), owned by Mr. O. Durand from Hoboken. The second Grand Prix of Belgium took place in 1928 and was won by Monarque, a son of Sadi and Samox.

Figure 2.26 The Malinois bitch Réséda (LOSH 10065), born May 1, 1920, and owned by Mr. L. Bekaert, was the major prize winner of the international tracking competition in Genk, Belgium, August 30–31, 1925. She was awarded the title of official champion by the Belgian FCI kennel club, KMSH.

In 1926 the Belgian Kennel Club—founded in 1908 by dissatisfied members of KMSH—held the ringsport championships. Two Malinois bitches took the top places: Ledy du Plateau won the Belgian championship, and in second place was Fidèle du Gallifort.

In 1929 Mr. J. Van Hooydonck's Balkhus du Gallifort became Belgian champion, and one year later he was second, and in 1931 third. He picked up the pace in 1932, when he won KMSH's Grand Prix of Belgium under the name Balkus (LOSH 39623). And in 1932, Balkhus du Gallifort took second in the Belgian Kennel Club championship. But 1933's championship saw a new winner: Capi de la Soierie, a Malinois owned by Mr. Malaise from Brussels.

From 1934 to 1937, the Malinois Snap van den Leeuw, owned by Mr. H. Van Leeuwen from Deurne, was champion. Of the 16 dogs participating in the final of the 1934 championship, 12 of the participating dogs were Malinois.

During the war years (1941–1943), KMSH's Grand Prix of Belgium was won by Snap van de Molenbeek (LOSH 89871) owned by Mr. R. Verlinde. This male, born July 23, 1937, was the result of a very close 3–2 inbreeding with the male Snapy (LOSH 40371). Through both parents, Snap van de Molenbeek was a descendant of Snap (Fram de Jolimont) of Mr. H. Hanssen from Antwerp. In his father's line Snap van de Molenbeek was also a great-grandson of Balkhus du Gallifort.

After World War II

The years 1940–1945 were a trying time for all kennels, and the Malinois kennels were no exception. In fact, just as World War I disrupted Malinois breeding, so too, World War II caused the best Malinois producers of the interwar period to disappear. The period after the war, again, saw the re-establishment of Malinois breeding, during which time Felix Verbanck and his De l'Ecaillon kennel strongly advocated for both long- and short-haired Belgian shepherd dogs. Verbanck's Nervien de l'Ecaillon allowed him to continue competing and breeding. Sadly, Nervien died at four years of age. Pan des Pimprenelles and Taquine de l'Ecaillon, the mother of Xante de l'Ecaillon (by the Tervueren, Tjop de la Brigade), as well as Sarah van Veldekens (the mother of the celebrated Ultima de l'Ecaillon), were some of Verbanck's best Malinois. At the time, high-quality stud dogs were rare in the Malinois variety, which explains why Xante was the daughter of Tervueren Tjop de la Brigade (the long-haired grandson of the Malinois Ideal de l'Ecaillon and Ivan de l'Ecaillon). Little by little, however, the De l'Ecaillon kennel ceased production. Verbanck's retirement in 1950 forced him to surrender what remained of his kennel.

Figure 2.27 Good breeding programs are complicated and can be destroyed by the upset of war. During World War II, Mr. Felix Eugene Verbanck's kennel, De l'Ecaillon, lost its best reproducers. However, in 1939 Gladiateur de l'Ecaillon bred with the female Maline des Pimprenelles and brought Mr. Verbanck a litter of three males, including Nervien de l'Ecaillon, who at first allowed the breeder to continue his work but then died at the age of four years. In 1944 Mr. Verbanck repeated this combination, which produced another male, Solitaire de l'Ecaillon. In 1945 he bred Pan des Pimprenelles with Maline des Pimprenelles, which yielded two females, including Taquine de l'Ecaillon, who in 1948 became the mother of Xante de l'Ecaillon by the faun, long-haired Tervueren Tjop de la Brigade (grandson of Malinois Ideal de l'Ecaillon and Ivan de l'Ecaillon). Close to the end of the kennel's existence, in 1946, Mr. Verbanck bred Milord de la Clef des Champs with Sarah van de Veldekens, who brought forth a litter of six puppies, including the celebrated Ultima de l'Ecaillon, shown here.

Other important kennels during this time were Van de Reep and Van de Welkom. Flap (known as Blackie van de Welkom) is the foundation of the modern French Malinois bloodlines.

From 1950 to 1960, Belgium saw a noticeable decline in breeding of dogs in general. Despite a constant number of dressage lovers, the Malinois also suffered a major decline. Still, during that time, at the ringsport games and the Grand Prix of Belgium, the Malinois vanquished almost all competitors. For instance, in 1960, almost all 23 participants in the Grand Prix were Malinois.

Of course, some kennels continued to steadily produce fine Malinois. Champions Tibi, Rex, and Rachid were from the

Figure 2.28 It was summer in the mid-1960s in Belgium. Just as we reached the causeway from the woods, the flock walked towards us. The day was closing, and the animals were on their way to the fold. They did not pay attention to us, and suddenly we were in the middle of their progress: pounding hoofs, creaking bushes, sniffing, nibbling, bleating, and bell tinkling. The shepherd, dressed in no-nonsense cotton, had a sturdy cap on his head and walked steadily, with his dog, behind the flock.

Fraternité kennel, and champions Snap, Varak, Vabil, Sito, Gary, and Eros came from the Van de Molenbeek kennel. Champions Carack, Cabil, and Hab from the Van de Oewa kennel also rose to prominence.

In 1961 a club at Rixensart, a municipality located in the Belgian province of Walloon-Brabant, worked with the Deutsches Verband für Gebrauchshundesportvereine (DVG) (German Association for Working Dog Sports Clubs), to found an event that would compare dogs trained according to the German program with Belgian dogs trained according to the Belgian program. Two dogs emerged as first-class representatives of their respective programs: Dr. Robert Osswald's Rottweiler, Farro von Sophienbusch, and the typical Malinois Desire, owned by Mr. Selleslach. Desire won the Grand Prix of Belgium in 1959 in Tournai. When expressing his admiration for Desire that year, Osswald is quoted in

Chasse et Pêche as having said, "To bring a dog to such perfection in his execution of all the exercises of the heavy program, and to bring him to the pinnacle of his condition, one must spend a lot of time with him, and most dog lovers are not able to do this. For the rest, most trainers would not have a practical use for such an excellently trained dog, and only police and official guards could benefit from him."

The Mondioring Program

In the early 1980s, after a French ring final match in France, representatives from the Netherlands, Switzerland, Italy, Belgium, and Germany met in a hotel in the city of Metz to present and explain their country's respective dog sports. The result of this meeting was the formation of a universal dog training program called Mondioring. The program integrates methods from German Schutzhund, IPO, French Ring, Swiss Schutzhund, Dutch KNPV, and Belgian Ring.

Mondioring demands a high degree of discipline and concentration from both dog and handler. It requires a closed terrain, various items and materials, and at least one helper wearing a complete protective suit. The Mondioring program consists of three disciplines with an obligatory order: obedience, jumping, and protection work.

The debutants start in the third category, and they complete the exercises in the three disciplines in that category. After reaching a quorum, they transfer to the second category the next season. If they achieve a certain level of results in that second season, they move along to the most difficult (first) category. As the dogs progress through the exercises, they will encounter bait (food), both offered and scattered on the terrain. The dogs should not be distracted by it.

Although the dogs, mostly the Malinois, are determined according to a defined program, the circumstances in which the

Figure 2.29 The Mondioring program has three disciplines: obedience, jumping, and protection work. (*Onze Hond*/belgianringsport.be)

Figure 2.30 The IPO program (German: Internationale Prüfungs Ordnung) consists of three trials: IPO 1, IPO 2, and IPO 3, each level increasing in difficulty. Each trial always has three phases: Phase A: Tracking; Phase B: Obedience; and Phase C: Protection. (*Onze Hond* Archive)

exercises are performed are always different from match to match, which is what makes the Mondioring discipline simultaneously beautiful and difficult.

When the dogs have completed the program of exercises, the jury judges the general attitude of dog and handler. A messy performance may cost a team additional points.

In total, 400 points can be earned. These points are divided as follows:

Obedience exercises: 60 points
Jumping exercises: 60 points
Protection exercises: 240 points
Food refusal: 20 points
General attitude: 20 points

Dogs participating in Mondioring must be free of genetic defects, of open-minded and balanced character, highly resilient, able to perform under pressure, full of temperament to very full of temperament, social to reasonably social, courageous under all circumstances, and confident with a natural sharpness (slightly irritable).

The Modern Era

To conclude this historical snapshot of the Malinois's development, we want to call attention to the important Belgian working kennels of the modern era: Van Boekhoutakker, Du Boscaille, Des Deux Pottois, Van de Duvetorre, Van de Haantjeshoek, Kukay's, Moulin Tombroeck, Van Rostenfoksen, and Van Joefarm. The last mentioned was an important kennel owned by Bertrand Vindevoghel and Nicky Van Gele from the end of the 20th century to the beginning of the 21st.

When Bertrand debuted his first Malinois in ringsport in the 1980s, he was instantly captivated by the breed. He achieved exceptionally good results with his dog, Joepy (Joe, for short). It didn't take long before there was a demand for Joe's offspring, and in October 1991 the first litter of Joepy and Inousca, a daughter of Belgian Work Champion (1983) and the first Mondioring World Champion (1987), Clip, was born. Due to the good results and the fine temperament of the puppies in that litter, demand increased. The kennel Van Joefarm thus began, and following are some of its important dogs.

Roe van Joefarm, a grandson of G'Bibber, participated in competitions in Belgian ringsport and Mondioring, with excellent results. He won many of these contests, partially because of his complete bite, which was one of his great attributes. Roe was twice selected for the Belgian ringsport championships (where he finished second) and three times for the World Cup Mondioring (finishing fourth). As a stud, he is world renowned. Many of his descendants have been successful in dog sports and as service dogs.

The Van Joefarm kennel bought Elgos du Chemin des Plaines from Luc Vansteenbrugge of the Des Deux Pottois kennel in 1995. They often used Elgos as a stud, and he brought added value to the kennel. Elgos was already well-known at home and abroad, not only because of his results in the ring but also because he proved himself as a stud. He is now found in many pedigrees as an ancestor and has hundreds of offspring. Elgos lives on in many people's thoughts to this day, a true legend in the Malinois world. When Van Joefarm acquired Elgos, they also bought Nelton des Deux Pottois. Nelton wasn't a social dog, as he had spent most of his life as a stud. The wildest stories about him circulate—"cleaning up" a dancefloor on his own; being thrown out a window and going right back to continue his work; biting under water. Nelton was greatly loved by surveillance people, police, practitioners of the KNPV (Royal Dutch Police Dog Association) program, and so on. His offspring usually inherited his confident character, his full grip, and his

Figure 2.31 G'Bibber, a son of Cartouche and Youri, born in 1981, was bred by Mr. Marc de Wilde. He came from the kennel Des Deux Pottois, operated by Mr. Luc Vansteenbrugge, and he put his stamp on the Malinois breed in Belgium and France, producing multiple working champions. (*Hondensport & Sporthonden*/Theo Dijkman)

Figure 2.32 Elgos du Chemin des Plaines, born in 1989 and bred by Mr. Jean Francois Gallais, was on his father's side a grandson of G'Vitou des Deux Pottois. He was first owned by Mr. Luc Vansteenbrugge, but was purchased by Van Joefarm in 1995. A grandson of G'Bibber, Elgos passed along outstanding qualities to his offspring. (*Hondensport & Sporthonden*/Theo Dijkman)

slightly "tough" look. His most famous successor was undoubtedly Urosh van Joefarm.

Urosh van Joefarm was son of Nelton and Sjoegar van Joefarm (a daughter of Elgos). Like his father, Urosh was a strong dog with a dominant character, without being aggressive. He was a typical

Figure 2.33 Yagus van de Duvetorre, bred by Johan Weckhuyzen in 1999, is, through his father Stoned van de Duvetorre, a grandson of Elgos du Chemin des Plaines. He, with owner and handler Mario Verslype, was FCI-World Champion 2003, FMBB Belgian Shepherds World Champion 2005, and FCI-World Champion 2005. (*Hondensport & Sporthonden*/Theo Dijkman)

alpha male, always looking to improve his place in his pack. Urosh was difficult to control because of the strength of his urges. However, he had a strong, full grip, and he was born to take care of business. And what he took care of, nobody touched! He was also a very good jumper—without muss or fuss, he could jump 4.3 feet (1.3 m).

Cjoe van Joefarm was born on November 13, 2003, the son of Roe van Joefarm and mother Abbata van Joefarm, a daughter of Elgos du Chemin des Plaines and granddaughter of Lucas des Deux Pottois, the son of the famous dog G'Bibber. Cjoe was a very fast dog with a full grip and great intensity. He was educated in the IPO program. Cjoe liked to take big leaps into the water, over and over again!

Devil van Joefarm was born on March 22, 2004, son of Yagus van de Duvetorre, a great-grandson of Elgos du Chemin des Plaines. Devil's mother, Arva van Joefarm, is a daughter of Roe van Joefarm x Yellow van Joefarm, a daughter of Elgos du Chemin des Plaines, so Devil is 3–3 inbreeding on Elgos. Devil is a dark dog with a phenomenal bite.

Fidirex van Joefarm (Cjoe's son), born on September 1, 2006, worked with his handler Mr. Rob Valk to become Dutch IPO champion in September 2009. He is a confident dog with a great temperament, highly intense with a fine work ethic. His bites are phenomenal. With his charisma, he stands head and shoulders above all the others. In the late 2000s, kennel co-owner Nicky wrote: "It's been years since a Malinois could tempt us so much! Not only is he very pure in the head, he shows not an ounce of aggression and is very confident in all circumstances. His work is driven by instinct, which makes it simple for him to do his job well. He doesn't only bite the IPO sleeve but also has no problem with a KNPV suit or a ringsuit. Many of his ancestors have monstrously big names: Cjoe (father), Roe (grandfather), Lucas des Deux Pottois, G'Bibber, Castor von Kronenburg, Cartouche, Arat, Educo, Missouri, Cabil, Sirol, Ecapi...too many known names in this bloodline to allow Fidirex to be a coincidence."

Best Working Dogs

Throughout the history of the Belgian sheepdogs, there have been two factions of enthusiasts: show lovers who have fierce ideas about coat colors and hair types, and the trainers who are not at all or hardly interested in the appearance of their dogs.

In the end, today's Malinois lovers must remember the words of Louis Huyghebaert, written in 1926: "The Malinois enthusiasts had a completely different view of the sheepdog. First of all, this had to be a working dog. The exterior aspect was not the main point in breeding but had to match his character. In other words, one selected talented working dogs who at the same time were well-formed, and who had an alert and intelligent mind. The color of the coat is only of additional importance. It is important that breeders always choose the most beautiful of the best working dogs."

3

Working Malinois in the Netherlands

Belgium, France, and the Netherlands all played a role in the development and evolution of the Malinois. It has become an outstanding working dog, not only in a sporting context but also in terms of police and patrol work.

In the 1980s, the Dutch kennel Van den Oudenakker, owned by Mr. L. Heuvelmans, produced the necessary beauty champions but also always bred excellent working Malinois. Oudenakker's breeding program was reflected in the kennel's many dogs with IPO (Internationale Prüfungs-Ordnung, or Schutzhund Training) and Royal Dutch Police Dog (KNPV) PH (Politie Hond, or Police Dog) certificates.

At about the same time, Mr. Harrie Verbakel bought for his Lianique's kennel the Malinois bitch Fencha van 't Rodolfsheim, who successfully produced several litters. He also bought the Malinois bitch Evelien van de Hoefaert, who at the 1981 World Dog Show in Dortmund became world champion. In 1981 Verbakel acquired an adult Malinois bitch named Dracka (LOSH 428286) from Heuvelmans's Van den Oudenakker kennel. Dracka was the granddaughter of Snap van Bouwelhei, and her father's side comprised many Belgian ringsport dogs. One of Dracka's daughters is Lianique's Arca (with father Ajax du Maugré), who became Dutch

Champion. Like Heuvelmans, Verbakel connected his breeding program with KNPV training.

KNPV IN THE 21ST CENTURY

Normally each dog certifies in his own province, and because of that, every year the KNPV holds several certification trials in each province to select the candidates for the KNPV National Championships. The decoys and the judges for each provincial trial are designated by the national KNPV office and always come from another province (they are never local and biased).

At this writing, each year, during the first weekend in September, the KNPV National Championships are held in the city of Eindhoven's soccer stadium (formerly it was held in the city of Hertogenbosch–Den Bosch, the Netherlands). The National Championships include a

- Police Dog 1 (PH-1) Championship, open to the ten highest-scoring dogs obtaining their PH-1 certificate that year. This means a dog can compete for the National Championship only once in his life.
- Police Dog 2 (PH-2) Championship, open to the highest-scoring PH-2 dogs from each of the 11 provinces of the Netherlands and the national champion from the previous year.
- Object Guarding Championship, open to the eight highest-scoring dogs of the year.

Figure 3.01 KNPV's training and certification method guarantees excellent police dogs. Many certified KNPV-trained dogs find work in police forces, customs, the military, and security companies in the Netherlands and abroad. This picture was taken at the KNPV National Championship in 2009. (*Onze Hond* Archive)

Figure 3.02 During the KNPV National Championships, always held during the first weekend of September, there are always many spectacular examples of police work, especially protection and bite work, as shown in this image from 2010. (Onze *Hond* Archive)

Legendary Malinois

In his magazine *Hondensport & Sporthonden* (*Dog Sport & Sporting Dogs*), editor-in-chief Theo Dijkman wrote a captivating and informative article about legendary Malinois in the Netherlands. With his permission, we include the entirety of this 1997 article here. For your information: KNPV normally place the owner's name in parentheses behind the dog's name.

LEGENDARY WORKING MALINOIS IN THE NETHERLANDS AND THEIR HISTORIC BLOODLINES: A DUTCH RETROSPECTIVE FROM THE 1960s TO THE 1990s

THEO DIJKMAN

Some of today's working breeds have rich and long histories. Almost 100 years ago, the Malinois originated from practical needs in daily life, namely the herding of sheep and the protection of these sheep against predators. At the end of the 19th century there were several sheep-herding dog breeds active in Belgium.

These dogs had a lot of passion for their work and were also a bit reserved toward people. The latter characteristic made them extremely suitable to function as guardian and defense dogs. In 1891 people tried to stimulate the breeding of these dogs with pedigree. About eight years later, four varieties of the Belgian shepherd dog were born: the Belgian sheepdog (Groenendael), the Belgian Tervueren, the Belgian Laekenois, and the Belgian Malinois.

Belgium, the Netherlands, and France are the countries in which this outstanding breed has developed. The Malinois has become an outstanding working dog, not only for sporting but also as a practical police and patrol dog.

In this article, we will discuss legendary Dutch Malinois from the 1960s through the 1990s, as well as their bloodlines.

REGISTERED AND MIXED MALINOIS

André Noël, owner of the well-known French kennel De la Noaillerie, and in my personal view a very important and highly respected connoisseur, once expounded on the reason why the Malinois is so outstanding as a working dog: "The reason for the supremacy of the Malinois is that this breed has always been a working breed. The Malinois is made by and for handlers." Compared to the dog's story in France, the history of the Dutch Malinois is very different. From the breed's beginning, only registered Malinois were bred in France. The Netherlands is the only country where mixed Malinois were also bred. And the mixed Malinois has been employed more within the KNPV (Royal Dutch Police Dog Association), and the professional sector, than the registered one.

One of the reasons for this was the awkward financial position of the Dutch dog handler directly after World War II. There was only enough money for daily needs. The name of a kennel from those days says it all: De Laatste Stuiver [The Last Penny]. Everything had to be as cheap as possible, and people did not want to lay out extra money to register pedigrees, even if both parent dogs were in the possession of a pedigree.

Another reason for this championing of the mixed Malinois is the culture of the KNPV training program. The handlers did not recognize any surplus value to using registered Malinois. Thus, the mixed Malinois has proven his value in the KNPV training program, but, especially over the last few years, more and more registered Malinois appear on the KNPV training fields. As well, the results of the KNPV Nationals—the Dutch National Championships for police dogs that provide the yearly highlights of the KNPV program—show

Figure 3.03 Mr. Hans van Rossum's Ika earned 100 points in tracking, 93 points in obedience, and 99 points in protection for a total of 292 points (out of a maximum 3 x 100 = 300 points). She became Dutch All Breeds Champion in 1993. (Halusetha's Kennel)

that registered Malinois are some of the best. Only one dog can qualify for the Nationals from each of the Netherlands' provinces, proving that registered Malinois fully competes with the mixed.

In 1998 there were four registered Malinois among the competitors. One must consider also that were several very good registered Malinois who were just one point away from selection for the KNPV Nationals. In 1998 Mr. Nico Poen and his registered Malinois Tjek even became Dutch Champion PH-1. Main conclusion: a registered Malinois is in no way inferior to the mixed one. Insiders with lots of experience even forecast an increasing use of registered Malinois in the KNPV program.

IPO–SCHUTZHUND

Registered Malinois have the upper hand over the mixed Malinois in the IPO training program. Mixed Malinois are not often seen in the IPO ranks because of the official FCI rule that allow only Malinois with pedigree at the championships. Competing with a mixed Malinois in IPO matches can only be done at regional matches. (From now on in this article, when we talk about the Malinois, we mean the registered Malinois with pedigree.)

The Malinois has dominated the yearly All Breeds Championship in the Netherlands. More than once, only Malinois have occupied the stand. Since

Figure 3.04 Mr. Frans Janssen and Arco earned 98 + 97 + 99 = 294 points to become Dutch All Breeds Champion in 1994; 100 + 97 + 99 = 296 points to become Dutch All Breeds Champion in 1995; and 100 + 97 + 97 = 294 points to become Dutch All Breeds Champion in 1998. Arco is the son of Bronco Perle de Tourbière (Mr. Jan Tinnemans) and Cobra van Tasca's Home. (*Hondensport & Sporthonden*/Theo Dijkman)

the 1990s, a long series of victories for Malinois in the Dutch IPO All Breeds Championship started. Mr. Hans van Rossum launched the series in 1993 with his bitch Ika. Mr. Frans Janssen then won in 1994, 1995, and 1998 with his Malinois dog Arco (bloodline: Eik des Deux Pottois), a son of the well-known Bronco Perle de Tourbière. In 1996 Mr. Fred Tichelaar with his Malinois Robby, a brother of Ika from the same litter, became Dutch All Breeds Champion. Robby and Ika immediately descended from Joerie and Ika des Deux Pottois.

Handlers like Fred Tichelaar (Malinois Robby, bloodline: Joerie and G'Vitou des Deux Pottois), Hans and Sonja van Rossum (Malinois Halusetha's Igor, bloodline: Eik des Deux Pottois and Joerie), and Erik Köpp (Malinois Tico van het Stokeind, bloodline: Eik des Deux Pottois), all dominated in the all-breeds IPO-III competitions of the mid- to late 1990s.

The world championship for Belgian shepherds hosted by the Fédération Mondiale du Berger Belge (FMBB) (World Federation for Belgium Shepherds) has been going since 1995. In 1997 Mr. Fred Tichelaar and Robby, Mr. Frans Janssen and Arco, Mrs. Sonja van Rossum and Halusetha's Igor, Mr. Erik Köpp and Tico van het Stokeind, and Mr. Rob de Heus and Pinto, with coach Theo Dijkman, won a beautiful second place during the third World Championship for Belgian Shepherds in Austria. In 1998 Van Rossum and Halusetha's Igor became world champion and the whole Dutch team achieved the same. All these dogs have distinctive bloodlines.

WORKING MALINOIS IN THE NETHERLANDS 73

Figure 3.05 Mr. Hans van Rossum's Ika and Mr. Fred Tichelaar's Robby stood several times in the second- and first-place spots on the podiums. In 1996 Tichelaar and Robby earned 96 + 97 + 98 = 291 points to become Dutch All Breeds Champion in 1996. (Halusetha's Kennel)

Figure 3.06 Eik des Deux Pottois (Mr. Bert Lamers) was born August 25, 1980, in the Des Deux Pottois kennel owned by Mr. Luc Vansteenbrugge. Eik's father was Oscar "Jalk" (Mr. K. Berkelaar) and his mother was Donna (Mr. D. Van der Wal). He was an important dog during his era. (*Hondensport & Sporthonden*/Theo Dijkman)

PIONEERS IN REGISTERED MALINOIS

A small number of Malinois in the Netherlands have played an important role in establishing the breed's current-day supremacy as a working dog in several programs. Famous names include Nopi, Narcilo, Kastor van de Rita's Home, Marco and Marko van de Veldmolen (from the same litter), Carlo van Kristalhof, Joerie, and Eik des Deux Pottois. Without doubt, someone will come up with another name to add to this list, but check your long-period pedigree and you will agree that the dogs mentioned above have laid the foundation for today's working Malinois in the Netherlands. Persons related to this foundation include Bert Lamers, Hans van Rossum, Theo Lemmers, Willem Gepken, Jan Tinnemans, and Mart Bos. Of course, there are many other names from the 1990s, and it's not our purpose to neglect them, but here we are talking about the decades leading up to the 1990s.

The names of the dogs mentioned above are seen (on the fourth, fifth, or higher lines) on almost 100 percent of Dutch pedigrees. If you have doubts: check your pedigree, specifically the lines before the ones that are printed.

In particular, Cabil (father of Nopi, grandfather of Narcilo, Marco and Marko van de Veldmolen, and great-grandfather of Kastor van de Rita's Home and Carlo van Kristalhof) has been very important for today's bloodlines, just like his son Narcilo.

Other important super-inheritance dogs are Bicou and G'Vitou des Deux Pottois. G'Vitou was the son of the legendary Clip, multiple champion of Belgium. Bicou also has Belgian parents.

Table 3.1 Super-Inheritance Malinois in the Netherlands

Name of Malinois	Date of Birth	Father	Grandfather	Great-Grandfather
Cabil	November 30, 1953	Sirol		
Nopi	February 4, 1964	Cabil		
Narcilo	May 12, 1964	Gladdy van de Purpere Heide	Cabil	
Kastor van de Rita's Home	March 16, 1969	Narcilo		Cabil
Carlo van Kristalhof	October 6, 1973	Narcilo		Cabil
Marco van de Veldmolen	January 15, 1972	Nopi	Cabil	
Marko van de Veldmolen	January 15, 1972	Nopi	Cabil	
Joerie	August 27, 1983	Dekx		
Bicou	July 28, 1977	Traf		

The pedigree of IPO-III world champion Halusetha's Igor (Sonja van Rossum) is an outstanding example. When you look at this dog's family tree, you find several of the names we have already mentioned.

Figure 3.07 Cabil (LOSH 166742) was born November 30, 1953, in Belgium. His father was Sirol (parents: Ecapi de Grand Rabot and Raak) and his mother was Ymbertine (Rachid de la Fraternité and Vinelle). (*Hondensport & Sporthonden*/Theo Dijkman)

Figure 3.08 G'Vitou des Deux Pottois (LOSH 476115), born February 16, 1982, was a dog with "two pedigrees." His true pedigree denotes his sire as Cartouche (Mr. M. de Wilde from Aalst, Belgium) and dam as Josque. Oddly, his pedigree papers are erroneous, denoting his father as Clip (LOSH 412720) and his mother as Dolie des Deux Pottois. G'Vitou was a medium-sized, robust male with a strong head, and he sired many important offspring. (*Hondensport & Sporthonden*/Theo Dijkman)

Table 3.2 Bloodlines of IPO-III World Champion, 1998, Halusetha's Igor

Name	Notable Grandparents	Notable Great-Grandparents
Halusetha's Igor	Eik de Deux Pottois	G'Vitou des Deux Pottois
	Joerie	Dekx
		Joenda (daughter of Bicou)
		Remy-Lea van het Baantje (daughter of Carlo van Kristalhof)

Figure 3.09 Halusetha's Igor was born November 13, 1990. His father was Brutus, owned by Mr. M. Smeijer, whose parents were Eik des Deux Pottois and Anoeska van het Askaremshof. His mother was Ika (Mr. Hans van Rossum) whose parents were Joerie and Ika des Deux Pottois. The team consisting of Sonja van Rossum and Halusetha's Igor was World IPO Champion in 1998. (Halusetha's Kennel)

Figure 3.10 Halusetha's Igor and Sonja van Rossum in the IPO obedience exercise, Retrieve Over a Hurdle. (Halusetha's Kennel)

The descendants from Fred Tichelaar's Robby are mainly found in the IPO circuit. He was used by the well-known kennels Halusetha's, Van Fort Oranje, and Van 't Haagse Bloed. Robby was five times a participant in the Dutch IPO All Breeds Championship, and was three times at the stand and one time a winner; he also participated three times in the World Championship for Belgian Shepherds and obtained the PH-1 certificate *met lof* [with honors].

WORKING MALINOIS IN THE NETHERLANDS

Figure 3.11 Robby, owned by Mr. Fred Tichelaar in Amsterdam, had Joerie (Mr. Spranger, Almere, the Netherlands) as a father and Ika des Deux Pottois (from the breeder M.M.L van Steenbruggen, Tournai, Belgium) for a mother. Ika was a daughter of G'Vitou des Deux Pottois. (Halusetha's Kennel)

Table 3.3 Bloodlines of the 1998 Dutch Malinois National Winners in KNPV and IPO

Name	Bloodlines
Tjek (PH-1 winner, 1998)	G'Vitou des Deux Pottois (2x), Clip
Arco (IPO-III All Breeds winner, 1994, 1995, 1998)	Eik des Deux Pottois, Dekx, Carlo van Kristalhof, Kastor van de Rita's Home, Marko van de Veldmolen, Narcilo, Nopi, Cabil
Banjer (Dutch Malinois National winner, 1998)	Eik des Deux Pottois, Joerie, Marco van de Veldmolen
Robby (PH-1 and IPO-III All Breeds winner, 1996)	Joerie, Dekx, G'Vitou, Clip

Interesting descendants of Robby include members of the A-litter Van het Eldenseveld from the bitch Bila Beau van de Ruisdael (granddaughter of Larco Perle de Tourbière and daughter of Amiga van Joefarm; the fifth-generation Robby of Mr. Fred Tichelaar) and from Koos van 't Haagse Bloed (the third-generation Robby of Mr. Fred Tichelaar). The dog Alix van het Eldenseveld of Mr. Jan van de Visch was three-time IPO-III Dutch Champion (2012–2014) and IPO Dutch all-breeds champion in 2014.

Figure 3.12 Part of the Dutch team at the first IPO World Championship organized by Fédération Mondiale du Berger Belge (FMBB) in 1995 at Bredene, Belgium. From left to right: Jan Hansum with Halusetha's Mac, Peter Verhoeven with Banjer van de Wierickerschans, Fred Tichelaar with Robby, Sonja van Rossum with Halusetha's Igor, and Frans Jansen with Arco. (Halusetha's Kennel)

Figure 3.13 Mr. Jan van de Visch's dog Alix van het Eldenseveld (Koos van 't Haagse Bloed x Bila Beau van de Ruisdael) was three-time Dutch IPO-III Champion (2012–2014) and Dutch All Breeds IPO Champion in 2014. He is a tough, dark dog that likes tracking and obedience exercises, and in protection work he has hard grips. Alix comes from old and established Dutch lines. (*Onze Hond* Archive)

Figure 3.14 Akira van het Eldenseveld is Alix's sister. She was nicknamed Google because she worked like a search engine. Her owners, Resi Gerritsen and Ruud Haak, ensured she possessed all possible search and rescue certificates, including the Mission Readiness Test Rubble (MRT). In this image she is working with her handler, the author, Ruud Haak.

Alix's litter sister Akira van het Eldenseveld (nicknamed Google because she worked like a search engine), owned by the authors, Dr. Resi Gerritsen and Ruud Haak, was in possession of all possible search and rescue certificates, including the Mission Readiness Test Rubble (MRT). She worked on lots of real area and rubble searches with the Austrian Red Cross.

By the way, the Malinois Novak du Boscaille (winner of several national IPO contests during the first half of the 1990s) seems to be the exception who proves the rule. That is, none of the dogs mentioned before seems to appear on the pedigree of this Belgian-made Malinois. But, if you study and go back far enough in his pedigree, you'll find the name of the well-known French Malinois Qu'rack du Bois D'Emblise, and it won't surprise you if I mention that Qu'rack is also in the fifth line of Halusetha's Igor! So, all lines came together to produce a superb working dog, the Malinois!

Influential Kennels

HALUSETHA'S

The Dutch kennel Halusetha's, owned by Hans and Sonja van Rossum, was famous for working Malinois in the late 1990s. They obtained many titles with Halusetha's Igor (son of Ika), but other dogs from their kennels were also at the highest level. Mr. Berry Kleinhesselink became the 1997 Dutch Champion with Halusetha's Nesch, and Mr. Willem den Oudsten became Dutch Champion in 2000 with Halusetha's Donder, a son of Snake (daughter of Robby) and Lando. Donder was also a multiple World Cup participant.

After breeding a litter, the bitch Snake was sold to the Danish kennel Daneskjold, where she became the ancestor of that kennel, bringing many very successful offspring both in sport and breeding. Daneskjold bought several dogs from Halusetha's, including Halusetha's Bobby (grandson of Ika and son of Robby) who became Scandinavian IPO-III Champion in 1997, 1998, and 2000. He also gained second place in the IPO-III championship for all breeds in Denmark two times, and he participated six times in Denmark in the World IPO-III Championship.

Figure 3.15 Halusetha's Igor was, like all Halusetha's dogs, a strong dog with a high drive who really liked to work. (Halusetha's Kennel)

Figure 3.16 Halusetha's Bobby (Robby x Halusetha's Pukkie Dulfer, a daughter of Mr. Van Rossum's Lando and Ika) came to reside at Finn Bertelsen and Margit Jensen's Daneskjold kennel in Denmark. Finn and Bobby were Scandinavian IPO-III Champion in 1997, 1998, and 2000; they were also two-time Danish IPO-III All Breeds Vice-Champion and represented Denmark six times as participants at the World IPO-III Championships. (Halusetha's Kennel)

Dr. Resi Gerritsen and Ruud Haak's Halusetha's Be Speedy was a litter sister of Bobby. Speedy had IPO-III certification and was fully trained in all-around search and rescue (SAR), including avalanche search work. She was Hungarian, Austrian, and Czech Search and Rescue Champion and was, in Ljubljana, with her

Figure 3.17 One of Bobby's litter sisters was Halusetha's Be Speedy, born April 30, 1994, and owned by Dr. Resi Gerritsen and Ruud Haak. Speedy achieved all IPO-R rescue and avalanche dog diplomas, was the 1997 World Vice-Champion Search and Rescue Dog in Berlin, and, with her team in Ljubljana, was 1999 World Champion Search and Rescue Dog. In addition, she was Hungarian, Austrian, and Czech Champion SAR Dog. In the field she showed her true mettle, especially when working many regional searches and major earthquake disasters in Turkey (1999), and in Algeria and Iran (2003). She saved 31 human lives.

Figure 3.18 In Ljubljana, a team of three Halusetha's dogs (left to right: Halusetha's Be Speedy, Halusetha's Igor Jr., and Halusetha's Karma) was given the 1999 World Champion Search and Rescue Dog award.

team of three Halusetha's dogs (Speedy, Karma and Igor Jr.), the 1999 World Champion SAR Dog. She was also used in many real searches regionally and in major earthquake disasters in Turkey (1999), Algeria, and Iran (2003). In this work, she saved 31 human lives.

Figure 3.19 Mr. Hans van Rossum's Lando was born February 15, 1990, to parents Arco Perle de Tourbière (Othar de la Noaillerie x Wanda) of Mr. Mart Bos, and Van Rossum's own Halusetha's Bianca (Joerie x Halusetha's Quinta). (Halusetha's Kennel)

Halusetha's Silex (Halusetha's Aico and Ika) was also a trained SAR dog. He participated four times in the World Championships and had IPO-III certification. However, he has no descendants.

PERLE DE TOURBIÈRE

Mr. Jan Tinnemans's active kennel, Perle de Tourbière, is a pioneer in the field of pedigreed Malinois, especially in the KNPV. Tinnemans started breeding his character Malinois more than 40 years ago. Well-known dogs include Bronco Perle de Tourbière (an excellent stud dog and son of Eik des Deux Pottois), Arco Perle de Tourbière (father of Lando of Mr. Hans van Rossum), Othar Perle de Tourbière, and Larco Perle de Tourbière. Several dogs from this kennel were very successful in IPO training, such as frequent World Cup–participant Igor Perle de Tourbière of Mr. Jo Slangen. IPO champion Arco was a son of Bronco Perle de Tourbière. Tico van het Stokeind of Mr. Erik Köpp was a son of Arco Perle de Tourbière. Tinnemans's Malinois have been famous for decades in the KNPV training program. The kennel has a reputation for excellent purebred Malinois suitable for this training and the heavy tasks performed by service dogs.

Figure 3.20 Bronco Perle de Tourbière was born April 23, 1986, to parents Eik des Deux Pottois and Wanda. Breeder Mr. Jan Tinnemans recalls, "At the time, I had Rudy, a pedigreed dog with a family tree from a good bloodline (Boscaille), so I was looking for a suitable bitch, who turned out to be Debora, a daughter of Carlo van Kristalhof (from Bert Lamers). From this litter I kept one bitch, Wanda. When I bred Wanda with Eik des Deux Pottois, Bronco Perle de Tourbière was born; and when I bred Wanda with Andre Noël's Othar de Noaillerie, they produced Arco Perle de Tourbière." (*Hondensport & Sporthonden*/Theo Dijkman)

Figure 3.22 Larco Perle de Tourbière was born in 1992 in Mr. Jan Tinnemans's kennel and comes from Bronco Perle de Tourbière and Stormy van de Drijvershoeve, a daughter of Arco Perle de Tourbière. Larco became the father of the famous Igor Perle de Tourbière. (*Hondensport & Sporthonden*/Theo Dijkman)

Figure 3.21 Mr. Jan Tinnemans's Speedy was a son of Berry, owned by Mr. Frijns. Speedy was the National Dutch KNPV Object Guarding Champion in 1988. (*Hondensport & Sporthonden*/Theo Dijkman)

Figure 3.23 In 1997 Igor Perle de Tourbière (Larco Perle de Tourbière x Jill Perle de Tourbière), owned by Mr. Jo Slangen, was twice National Champion in the Dutch Championship of Belgian Shepherds. He came in second at the 2003 IPO World Championship in Wavre, Belgium, and third at the 2003 FMBB World Championship in De Haan, Belgium. (*Hondensport & Sporthonden/ Theo Dijkman*)

Figure 3.24 Othar Perle de Tourbière (father: Larco Perle de Tourbière, the son of Bronco Perle de Tourbière; mother: Siska Perle de Tourbière, whose paternal grandfather was Bronco Perle de Tourbière) was born in 1998 and is owned by Mr. T. Tijsseling. (*Hondensport & Sporthonden*/Theo Dijkman)

Figure 3.25 Fiërro Perle de Tourbière (Cody Perle de Tourbière x Bica Perle de Tourbière), bred by Mr. Jan Tinnemans in 2005 and owned by Mr. Theo Dijkman, has Larco Perle de Tourbière as a maternal grandfather *and* a paternal great-grandfather. (*Hondensport & Sporthonden/ Theo Dijkman*)

Mixed-Breed Malinois

Now some words about the development of all those excellent mixed-breed Malinois, especially in the Netherlands. World War II had serious consequences for the Malinois in Europe, but soon after that difficult time, breeding and training started again. But in contrast to Belgium and France, where most of the dogs were pedigreed, in the Netherlands the mixed-breed Malinois also became very popular. This mixed breed, called kruising Mechelse Herder (xMH for short) in Dutch, especially excelled in the training and breeding for the KNPV and the professional sector of service dogs.

In February 2000 Theo Dijkman wrote a great article about the mixed-breed Malinois, also in *Hondensport & Sporthonden*. With his permission, we include the entirety of this article here.

THE xMALINOIS IN KNPV DRESSAGE: TOP TRAINING WITH DOGS OF PROVEN BLOODLINES!

THEO DIJKMAN

KNPV training has a long and rich history because the Royal Dutch Police Dog Association was founded in 1907. Over the last decades, the Malinois has taken a leading position as a work horse in the KNPV. In contrast to his work in other disciplines, the Malinois's non-pure variant has proven his value here.

This article discusses the amazing and admirable role of a dog that is unmatched in KNPV training. True, we talk about dogs without pedigree but with excellent practical and proven bloodlines developed by highly experienced trainers. It's no coincidence that most of the current service dogs working in the police, military, customs, etc. originate from KNPV training. A dog with such a story can't be described in a few pages.

It is typical for the breeding lines of the Malinois in the KNPV, as well as the lines in the Belgian ring, to favor the working character. From the beginning, working character has been the most important factor in these dogs, and still is. The contribution of exterior show lines is nil, and because of that these dogs could strongly develop physically and mentally. Breeders have, from time to time, applied line breeding and inbreeding, and although this method of

Figure 3.26 Kiener (LOSH 197867) won the Saint-Hubert Grand Prix of Belgium in 1963 and then started at the NVBK, where he won the title three times. Kiener was very talented and intelligent but too big, which caused him back problems. He also had very big ears. Through his mother Criquette (LOSH 166749), Kiener was the grandson of the legendary Sirol, who had a great influence on today's working-dog lines. (*Hondensport & Sporthonden*/Theo Dijkman)

breeding can have an adverse effect if it is not used in a thoughtful manner, it has been demonstrated in practical terms that it can have great benefits.

Describing the origin of bloodlines of the dogs going through KNPV training is not easy. How far back in time, after all, was the first stone laid? Nevertheless, according to today's practice, many of the dogs currently working are derived from bloodlines of dogs that were in possession of legendary trainers and breeders such as Berkelaar, Derks, Hogeling, Thiel, Rossum, Lamers, and so on.

BREED BASIS

The foundation of many of these dogs comes from Belgium, the lines of Sint-Hubertus (KMSH) and the Nationaal Verbond van Belgische Kynologen (NVBK) [National Federation of Belgian Cynologists] . . . . Mr. Linders of Lanaken (Belgium) and his brother Toine were in possession of the best dogs in Belgium: Cabil and litter sister Criquette, Kiener and Frank. Mr. Jansen once said, "Kiener was like Eddy Merckx: He came, saw and conquered." And Kiener did exactly that on a Sunday in three matches in Belgian ringsport. (Note: Participating in multiple matches was, in principle, possible in the Belgian ring program in the 1960s.) In the first match, Kiener finished third, and in the other two matches he won. [Kiener, born 1961 and died 1975, was multiple Belgian champion of the Nationaal Verbond van Belgische Kynologen (NVBK). He was known for his size and intelligence, but that size also caused him back problems later in life.]

Figure 3.27 Oscar "Jalk" of Mr. Cees Berkelaar made an unforgettable impression in his bite work: high and hard as a rocket. He was literally a high flyer, who could jump at the decoy from 8 meters (26 ft) away, and make contact. Oscar serviced 420 bitches in the Netherlands and abroad, and has thus been of great influence! (*Hondensport & Sporthonden*/Theo Dijkman)

The descendants of Kiener have been of great influence, including Rex, owned by Mr. Van de Broek, and the dog Leon of Mr. Thijssen from Limburg who was the PH-1 champion in 1975. Reuver's Mr. Peeters's dog Narcilo was not big in size, but in his bite work Narcilo was a real giant. One of Narcilo's sons was Robbie, owned by Mr. Hoogenboom; he was several times a participant in the KNPV Championships and was PH-2 champion in 1975. Robbie's bite work was impressive; he had an incredibly hard bite. Carlo van Kristalhof was a brother of this dog (from a later litter). Carlo had a pedigree because his mother was already registered in the Dutch stud book (NHSB).

OSCAR, NOPI, AND BERRY

Another example of a dog with a strong inheritance was Mr. J.W. Bruinsma's dog Flapy (nicknamed Rex), who worked with the Rotterdam Police. This dog also had a Belgian pedigree, and one of the best-known sons of this dog is the very famous Oscar (nicknamed Jalk), owned by Cees Berkelaar. Oscar's bite work made an unforgettable impression; this dog bit high and hard as a rocket. He was literally a high-flyer who often jumped at the helper (and made contact) from 26 feet (8 m) away. During the 1970s and 80s, whoever in the Dutch province Zuid-Holland didn't have a dog with Oscar's "blood" did not really count. Oscar serviced 420 bitches in the Netherlands and abroad, and has thus been of great influence!

Nopi, the purebred Malinois of Mr. Lennartz from Maastricht, has also been of great value. This dog was nicknamed for his father, Cabil, who was owned by Mr. Jansen from Lanaken (Belgium).

Another important dog was Mr. Frijns's Berry. This dog was not big in size but in character. It's said that once a month Berry would revolt, after which his handler had to engage in a great struggle with his dog to gain control again. Berry became a reserve champion in 1972. He produced several good dogs, such as the well-known Prins of Mr. Leenders (PH-1 reserve champion), Speedy of Mr. Jan Tinnemans, and Nero of Mr. Kamps. A daughter of Berry was covered by Oscar, and that union produced the "superman" Roy of Mr. Eppink. Roy was famous for his great attack and was Dutch champion in 1987 and PH-2 reserve champion in 1989.

IMPORTANT BITCHES AND STUD DOGS

Of course, 1980 to 2000 also saw some very important bitches. For example, there was Astrid of Mr. W. van Breugel, who produced several dogs with certificates. A well-known son of Astrid was Arras, owned by Mr. Wiel Derks. The father of Arras was Mr. Derks's Marco, a dog with wonderful descendants that also inherited strong qualities. Astrid's ancestors included Marco of Mr. J.H. Weekers, a dog with the pedigree name Unok van de Oewas from a kennel in Lanaken owned by Mr. Jansen.

In most Dutch provinces there have always been a few leading stud dogs. For example, the province Limburg had Iwan of Mr. Christ van Thiel. Iwan had an unbelievably good attack. In Drenthe lived Mr. Kamps's Nero (son of Prins), Pecco of Mr. Pegge, and Berry of Mr. J.A. Hogeling (the latter was PH-1 champion in 1985). The dog Barry, owned by Mr. Willemsen from Tilburg, was renowned for his solid bloodlines; he serviced over 75 bitches.

INFLUENCE OF PUREBRED MALINOIS

As you know, some pedigree dogs have had a major influence on current Malinois in the KNPV. For instance, the legendary purebred Groenendael Andor van de Ijsselvloed, owned by Mr. Theo Berkers. Andor was PH-2 champion of the Netherlands in 1977, 1979, and 1980, and was well-trained. He serviced a total of 46 bitches, from whom the so-called Nero and Buddha lines come, black Malinois (also called crossed Groenendael) who were and are excellent workers. Andor is clearly the chief ancestor of today's black Malinois.

Figure 3.28 The pedigreed Groenendael dog Andor van de Ijsselvloed (Santa van 't Skepershoes x Astra), born March 23, 1973, and owned by Mr. Theo Berkers, was three-time KNPV PH-2 Champion (1977, 1979, and 1980). Andor is the ancestor of today's black Malinois within the KNPV training circle. (*Onze Hond* Archive)

Figure 3.29 The black xMalinois (abbreviated as xMH) Dico of Mr. R. Wammes participated in the KNPV Object Guarding National Championship in September 2000, at Den Bosch, the Netherlands. On his mother's side Dico is a descendent of Mr. J. Berkers's Buddha, who descends from Andor van de Ijsselvloed.

The coming together of Andor with a daughter of Kastor van de Rita's Home produced especially good dogs. The two best-known direct descendants of Andor—Nero and Buddha—produced many good dogs in combination with the lines of Iwan (Van Thiel) and Oscar (Berkelaar). Kastor van de

Rita's Home, owned by Mr. Bert Lamers, is another important dog to mention regarding the evolution of the working Malinois. Just like his father Narcilo, Kastor was known for his excellent bite work.

GREAT CHAMPIONS

The great Andor van de Ijsselvloed won several championships. The same was also achieved by some other dogs. Mr. Jansen's Nero, for example, was four times KNPV champion of the Netherlands. One of Nero's sisters, who showed great resemblance to a German shepherd dog, was covered by the Belgian champion dog Kiener (of Mr. Jansen from Belgium). From this combination came the famous Rex, owned by Mr. van de Broek.

Mr. Klaas Terpstra's Donna was unforgettable. She became three-time Dutch PH-2 champion (1991, 1992, 1993). Donna's father was Mr. Derks's Arras, mentioned above. Donna was covered by Mr. Hans van Rossum's Rambo, and that union produced excellent dogs such as Rudo, PH-1 champion (1993), owned by Mr. van Vulpen.

Rambo was another big champion. His influence on bloodlines is still commonly seen in today's litters. Rambo became the Dutch PH-2 and Object Guarding champion in 1990, and one year later he took second place in the PH-2 championship (behind Donna). Owners of the champion dogs of this era—Van Rossum, Terpstra, and Van Vulpen—were members of the same KNPV club. Rambo's father was the pedigreed Eik des Deux Pottois of Mr. Bert Lamers. On the mother's side, Rambo's lines include Prins (Mr. Leenders), Linda (Mr. Jan Tinnemans), and Berry (Mr. Frijns). Especially from bitches of the Arras line, Rambo's offspring were excellent workers.

Mr. Piet Mandemakers's dog Buck was one of Rambo's sons and entered several championships. Buck became the 1996 champion in KNPV Object Guarding. Another well-known son of Rambo was Bruno of Mr. C.B. van de Steen, who became Dutch PH-1 champion in 1995. Bruno's brother Kazan of Mr. van den Hoff from the same litter became the PH-2 reserve champion in 1995, and the entire litter, except for one, obtained a certificate. In 1999 Mr. van de Want was present at the PH-2 championship with another Rambo, named after his father. At this writing, at the beginning of the 21st century, the Mr. Henk Roelofs's dog Laron was the last dog to win the Dutch championship several times. Laron was excellent in all disciplines and became PH-2 champion in 1996, 1997, and 1998, and finished third in the PH-2 championship in 1999.

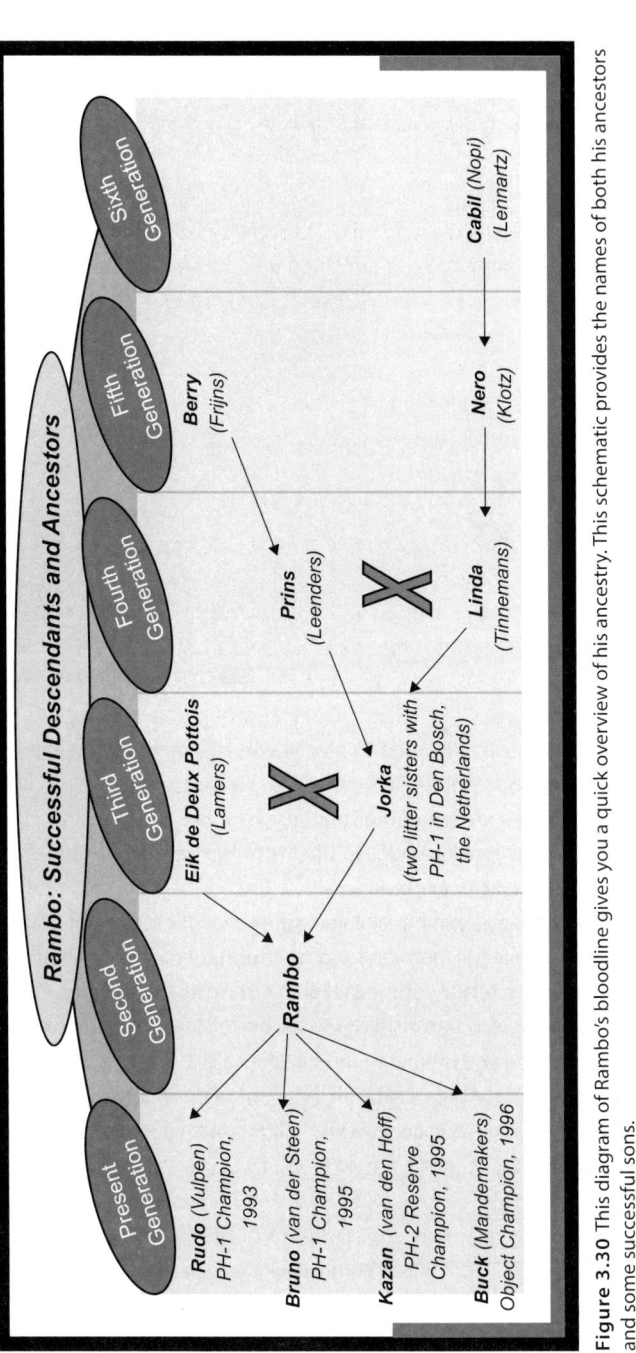

Figure 3.30 This diagram of Rambo's bloodline gives you a quick overview of his ancestry. This schematic provides the names of both his ancestors and some successful sons.

Figure 3.31 Mr. Hans van Rossum's Rambo, born of parents Eik des Deux Pottois and Jorka (Mr. Marcus), who was a daughter of Prins (Mr. Leenders) and Linda (Mr. Tinnemans). In 1990 Rambo was both KNPV National PH-2 Champion and KNPV National Object Guarding Champion. (Halusetha's Kennel)

In this article, we have tried to give you as complete as possible an overview of the development (up to 2000) of the xMalinois in the KNPV. Of course, it is impossible to write about the countless handlers and dogs that have contributed to all the excellent dogs in the KNPV. We have tried to record all the bloodlines as accurately as possible, although there is a chance that someone may have a different opinion, because some bloodlines are not 100 percent verifiable. If we have not mentioned some important names in this article, consider the extensive history of the Malinois. Listing all the people and dogs by name in a few pages is impossible, and we do not intend to hurt anyone who has contributed to the ultimate working dog: xMH—the Malinois without a recognized family tree but capable of excellent performance as a working dog and whose value is more than recognized by so many people in daily practice!

4

Behavior, Raising, and Training

Correct temperament is essential to a working Malinois. The breed is confident, exhibiting neither shyness nor aggressiveness when encountering new situations. The dog may be reserved with strangers but is affectionate with her own people. She is naturally protective of her owner's person and property without being overly aggressive. The Malinois possesses a strong desire to work and is quick in response to commands from her handler.

The Malinois's character is passionate but also stable and social when interacting with people, which cannot be said of many other modern breeds. However, for a Malinois and her handler to work well together, nuances in her character must be well-understood and interpreted.

Behavior in the Pack

From their ancient wolf ancestors, dogs possess attributes of vigilance, loyalty, and submission. In addition, dogs have strong social behaviors, which means they are driven to share their lives with others. Because humans have chosen to make dogs useful to them, we must understand their behaviors, social and submissive. These behaviors allow dogs to adapt well to the rules of the group, in most cases their human families.

Figure 4.01 Where early peoples and wolves in their many varieties lived together, dogs were slowly produced as pets. Young wolves were taken out of their dens and raised by people. Humans chose to domesticate and make useful those wolves who would live in the human pack. (Shutterstock/ Nagel Photography)

A pack of dogs is controlled by a social hierarchy, which is organized around a few important rules. For example, a strong dog will dominate a weaker dog, and an adult dog predominates a younger dog of similar size and strength. A female dominates a male of the same size and strength, because males are naturally disinclined to bite females. These are rather general rules, of course, and exceptions arise from individual courage, aggression, hardness, cowardice, and so on.

Once a dog's rank is established within the pack, it will remain relatively unchanged for a long time. From time to time, younger dogs will try to drive higher-placed dogs out of their positions. Rebellious youngsters, however, often cease this behavior when they encounter the higher-ranking animals making clear their positions via impressive behaviors, such as making themselves bigger by walking with tight legs and raising their hackles, snarl, snap, and even make sorties. All these shows of dominance provide clear signals to the lower-ranked animals: higher-ups do not take challenges lightly.

An adult dog can threaten a young dog but will never really attack her. The adult displays a natural bite inhibition with puppies. But how does an adult dog recognize puppies as "young"? Size is not the chief factor here, otherwise an adult dachshund would

BEHAVIOR, RAISING, AND TRAINING 95

Figure 4.02 Dogs inherited vigilance, loyalty, and submission behaviors from their ancestor, the wolf. In addition, the dog, like her ancestor, is an animal with strong social behaviors, which translates into a great willingness to share life with others. (Shutterstock/Nagel Photography)

Figure 4.03 From time to time, younger dogs will try to drive higher-placed dogs out of their positions. However, the rebellious youngsters soon stand down when they see impressive behavior like that displayed by the dog on the left in this picture.

not be able to recognize a young Malinois. Appearance, likewise, is not the measure, because the wide variety of breeds offers great diversity in body shapes. In the end, it is the puppy's behavior that signals her age to an adult dog. For example, as soon as a young dog feels threatened, she instinctively displays a submissive attitude. She will lie on her back and expose her throat and belly to the one posing the threat. Sometimes she will urinate a bit, and the higher-ranked dog will investigate this. All these behaviors encourage bite inhibition. Some dogs retain these puppy behaviors throughout their lives, but this is a sign of abnormal submission.

Figure 4.04 As soon as a young dog feels her safety is threatened, she instinctively displays a submissive attitude.

In the daily lives of all social animals, minor disputes arise. If every little quarrel became a serious fight, many members of the pack would be killed or seriously wounded. However, most internal conflicts are resolved without bloodshed. Dominant dogs usually follow their instincts for inhibition, which interrupt any attack. This way, fights end with the dominant behaviors as enough of a deterrent for upstarts. Near the end of altercations, lower-ranked dogs sometimes try to lick the lips of the dominant ones or they lick their own lips, and sometimes they yawn. These typical submissive gestures reconfirm dominant dog's position in the pack.

Differences in Behavior

Behaviors are a series of actions carried out by a dog after she receives a stimulus. The stimulus can be internal or external. A good example of an internal stimulus is feeling hungry, which prompts the dog to search for food. An external stimulus is the appearance of an approaching enemy, which initiates certain actions, such as flight or aggression. It has become clear that no dog responds to a stimulus in the same way. In fact, there are big differences in behavior, which vary not only by breed but also by individual.

For as many differences there are in canine behavioral responses to stimuli, there are human preferences for those behaviors. For example, some appreciate their dog's aggressive behavior, twigged by the slightest incentive, even brought on without an obvious reason. These dog owners are happy to keep their dog on short leash when meeting anyone, even a person or an animal well-known to the dog. Of course, there is a difference between dogs that really would bite even a well-known visitor and the owners who boast their dogs would. People often bluff about their dog's powers. Those whose dogs truly react sharply and aggressively must constantly be on the alert. When sharp dogs are not well-educated and supervised, they are a torment to their handlers and everything they touch.

Other people, like us, prefer quiet, reliable dogs who do not require constant vigilance, well-socialized dogs that can move in and out of any environment without causing a stir. These dogs stand their ground when the situation requires them to, but they can distinguish between playtime and a serious situation, and are the most enjoyable dogs one can imagine. These reliable dogs gently play with their family's children and those of strangers, but they also defend home and human if necessary.

On the opposite end of the spectrum from the aggressive dogs are the scared and shy ones. Afraid of their own shadows, they constantly feel surrounded by impending danger. And their behaviors show it. They are anxious about every strange situation and hide between their owner's legs when they approach strangers. They crouch at the least incident, such as a falling chair, and then take a wide berth around whatever caused the upset. Such dogs should not be bred, and they translate into despair for their owners. Fortunately, the Malinois can be counted as the stronger and more stable of the Belgian

Figure 4.05 Everybody who engages with Malinois must realize that these Belgian shepherds are not only beautiful and harmoniously built, but also working dogs. The most beautiful Malinois that takes fright at the slightest sound shames the breed.

shepherd varieties. One rarely encounters an inherently fearful Malinois.

Beauty and Work

When we consider how intelligently the Malinois works with sheep, and what achievements they are capable of in dog training, we can see the great qualities our ancestors saw as they carefully selected dogs for breeding, again and again. Everybody who engages with Malinois must realize that these Belgian shepherds are not only beautiful and harmoniously built, but also, at the foundation, working dogs. The beautiful Malinois that takes flight at the drop of a hat shames the breed. What the Malinois owner, handler, and enthusiast wants to see in his or her dog is clearly stated in the current breed standard of the Fédération Cynologique Internationale (FCI):

General Appearance: Belgian shepherd is a medio lineal dog, harmoniously proportioned, combining elegance and power; of medium size, with dry strong muscle, fitting into a square; rustic, used to the open-air life and built to resist the frequent atmospheric variations of the Belgian climate. Through the harmony of his shape and high head carriage, the Belgian shepherd should give the impression of the elegant strength that has become the heritage of the selected representatives of a working breed.
Behavior/Temperament: Belgian shepherd is a watchful and active dog, bursting with energy, and always ready to leap into action. As well as his innate skill at guarding flocks, he also possesses the highly prized qualities of the best guard dog of property. Without any hesitation, he is the stubborn and keen protector of his owner. He brings together all those qualities necessary for a shepherd, guard, defense, and service dog. His lively, alert temperament and confident nature, showing no fear or aggressiveness, should be obvious in his body stance and the proud, attentive expression in his sparkling eyes. When judging this breed, one should take into consideration his calm and fearless temperament.

The same breed standard also indicates the wrong behavior of the Belgian shepherd. Under "Faults," we read: "*Temperament:* Specimens lacking in self-confidence or overly nervous." And under "Disqualifying Faults": "*Temperament:* Aggressive or timid specimens." Any dog clearly showing physical or behavioral "abnormalities shall be disqualified."

Who Should Raise Malinois?

A good Belgian shepherd should be lively, full of energy, and above all curious. There are few things she doesn't observe, and she has a keen interest in everything that happens in her surroundings. The Belgian shepherd is constantly pursuing her handler, walking near the handler's feet, and wanting to see and notice everything.

Even when her handler sends her to her bed, her eyes follow all the handler's movements and things that happen around her. This is the type of dog who likes to be with her handler and the family, and wants to go with them everywhere. Those who cannot have an attentive, curious dog around them all day should not take on a Belgian shepherd. In addition to being an excellent service dog, the Malinois is a true family dog. She will certainly not like a day's stay in a kennel.

Sheepdogs make certain demands on the character and abilities of their owners. Owning sheepdogs has its challenges, and you really must love them to want to deal with them daily. Besides being attentive and sometimes demanding roommates, Malinois are working dogs who are motivated to perform certain tasks. They are busy and sometimes restless. In addition, many Malinois are what handlers and trainers call "soft dogs," sometimes also not very self-confident. A "soft dog" is quickly discouraged by harsh words spoken by her handler. Some Malinois immediately show submissive behavior when punished, so submissive that handlers can become hesitant to correct their dogs. An excessively submissive dog is difficult to raise properly. Usually, overly submissive dogs do not become good working dogs.

Malinois often make necessary demands on their handlers. Those who are flamboyant in nature, who like to dominate, should forget about training a Malinois. This personality type would mess up a Malinois in short order. Quiet people who have great patience for their dogs, as well as an understanding and knowledge of the Malinois, will find a good match with this dog, who can easily learn to be a good worker. Most Malinois take a while to mature. Dogs who remain young at heart for a long time should be treated as young dogs for a long time. Like puppies, young-acting Malinois adults do not bear the pressure of harsh or rough treatment. By the time they are two or three,

Figure 4.06 Most Malinois need a quite long time to grow up. They remain young at heart for a relatively long time and so should be treated as young dogs for a long time.

however, they will be mature, and then you can ask more of them. If you give them the support and confidence they need until they mature, they will prove to be indispensable to you. If, however, you train them too early, too often, and reprimand them too much when they are young, they are less likely to work well later. So, Malinois owners must have the appropriate character and should expend the necessary effort to properly educate their Malinois.

When we think about the unique characteristics of Malinois behavior and human response to that behavior, we also can't help thinking about breeders, judges, and breed clubs, which must target certain dogs for breeding to perpetuate acceptable characters, according to breed standards. We believe that the purebred Malinois and the Malinois crossbreeds that are specially designed for breeding working dogs still produce the character

Figure 4.07 The Malinois we see with the KNPV and in the Belgian and French ringsport programs can be counted among the very best, and they display desirable working-dog characteristics.

dogs that can deliver the same great performances as their ancestors. The Malinois we see with the KNPV and in the Belgian and French ringsport programs can be counted among the very best, and they display good examples of desirable working-dog characteristics.

BRED FOR WORK

For centuries, dogs were bred to work; the Malinois's job was with the flock or on the farm. Dogs that were not suitable for their work were killed or given away to people who did not breed dogs. Only the very best remained and were used for breeding. In beautiful interplay with farmer or shepherd, or even completely independently, those working dogs performed their jobs steadfastly and reliably. While this is true, do not imagine an idyllic relationship between shepherd and dog. The dogs rarely came inside their masters' homes and were bred to be working outside, shouldering their heavy workloads. The only measure of dogs for breeding was their fitness to work, and the behavioral characteristics that allowed them to do their jobs.

It's been more than a century since farms required the kind of working dogs the Malinois was designed to be. This change probably represents the biggest leap ever experienced by dogs after their domestication. As we urge so often in this book, and in our work with working dogs: let us be very careful that we do not, in our desire for beautiful "pet" dogs, create animals that are empty of skill and working character.

Raising a Malinois

Raising and training Malinois is different from doing the same with so many other kinds of dogs. The basic differences can be seen when they are puppies.

Most puppies observe what they want to see in their surroundings and take little notice of all the rest. They do not react to acoustic or environmental stimuli, which are not interesting for them. They are oriented to the people who are with them; that is the most important thing.

In contrast, the Malinois puppy sees and hears everything, and reacts to everything, even a bird flying over her. She always wants to be active, exploring every wonderful thing about her environment. Equally, she notices the things that aren't so wonderful—even frightening—and so, she can become skittish.

Second, while other puppies react neutrally or even with interest to a strange person, Malinois puppies may react with reserve and nervousness. Trying to engage a shy puppy will usually draw any other kind of puppy out of her shell, but not the Malinois, who instead becomes more withdrawn than before.

Third, when other puppies get tired, they stop what they're doing and have a rest. Malinois puppies do not. They go on and on until their handlers intervene and tell them it's time for a rest. It is important to remember that the busier the Malinois puppy,

Figure 4.08 Most puppies observe what they want to see in their surroundings and take little notice of all the rest. In contrast, the Malinois puppy sees and hears everything, and reacts to everything.

the more tired she is! Thinking she'll stop when she's tired is folly. A lot of people think, "Okay. If this puppy wants to keep running after the ball, she can't be tired." But this line of thinking can be fatal for a Malinois.

As a result, Malinois puppies must have regular rest, and in a quiet place, otherwise they don't sleep. If you put your puppy into a kennel, she will begin turning around in circles, reacting to every stimulus, and she will bark nervously. If you must use a kennel, put a crate or dog carrier into it, so your Malinois puppy can curl up in it and go to sleep.

A fourth difference lies in how puppies discover the world. For most puppies, discovery is an easy process: slowly, you introduce them to new parts of their world. Step by step, they learn about the things around them that interest them. As a result, their world feels safe and acceptable. If something happens to frighten them, you can support them by putting them on leash, taking them over to show them the problematic item, that there is nothing to worry about. Even off leash, you can lure them

Figure 4.09 It is important to remember that the busier your Malinois puppy, the more tired she is! It is important that you ensure she gets regular and sufficient rest.

over to the scary item with a ball or another toy. Using this method, you can shepherd puppies through many new, and even frightening, situations.

Malinois puppies are different because they want to know about everything around them, in depth. You should go everywhere with your puppy, so she can experience as much as possible with your support. Even as you allow her to explore, you must also ensure she has enough time to sleep to deal with all the new impressions.

When Malinois puppies become nervy or reserved, luring them out of their shell likely won't work. Instead, focus on your own behavior. Show a very confident attitude, walk on normally, and oblige your puppy to go with you. The more you try to cajole your puppy, the more she will refuse. Sometimes showing a toy or a ball will help to bring her through a scary situation. But, never use a

Figure 4.10 Employ a strict time schedule for eating, resting, training, and working. The better structured your Malinois's time, the higher the level of performance she will attain.

soothing voice or display some sort of reassuring behavior, because that will only ensure she stays nervous or reserved about whatever the problem is, and for a long time. The Malinois works really well with a no-nonsense approach.

Because the Malinois becomes overstimulated easily, it is important to structure her world from the beginning. Employ a strict time schedule for eating, resting, training, and working. The better structured her time, the higher the level of performance attained.

Fifth, the young Malinois is not only known for learning quickly but also for her tendency to become upset quickly if she doesn't understand. She can become very excited, almost as if she can't find the right spot in her mind for all her thoughts. When this happens, you must interfere and settle your dog by making it clear what exercise she must perform, showing her a logical approach, and not encouraging the dog with words.

In learning the different exercises, the young Malinois needs a fixed, clear, no-nonsense approach. Most of the time, the Malinois is passionate about many things at once—her different instincts will be firing on all cylinders—and she can be driven to distraction if she is not under control. Other young dogs mostly don't have so much drive, or so many drives engaged at once. If other dogs could speak, they would ask their handlers, "Tell me what to do now," as opposed to a Malinois, who would say, "I already know what to do now!" Because the Malinois is such a quick study, you must be careful. Other dogs may not pick up on faults in training, but a Malinois might just as easily pick up on the mistakes you make in training her, which you will have to eliminate later, through more training.

Training Problems

The Malinois is an active, even busy, dog, willing to work full-out but, because of her enthusiasm, is sometimes a bit difficult to work correctly. She is eager to learn but a bit sloppy. Good trainers and handlers tolerate the initial inaccuracies in training because a well-trained Malinois is an excellent working dog with a powerful and convincing bite and is easy to motivate in bite work.

The character of the Malinois is rather tough, which means that after a bad experience, the dog will recover her good temper and eagerness for the work after receiving a kind word from her handler. Unfortunately, her toughness can fool substandard handlers into being too hard on her, and thus giving her the wrong kind of education. Although she is tough, the young, growing Malinois is very sensitive to the attitude and moods of her handler and must be approached quietly and raised with the necessary sensitivity. If the handler is too rough, the Malinois will be ruined (becoming fearful, aggressive, or inaccessible to further training). If she is treated with dignity and sensitivity, however, she will develop into an excellent working dog.

You can see the differences between Malinois and other breeds as Malinois finish their training and are placed in service. Most

Figure 4.11 The Malinois's toughness can fool substandard handlers into being too hard on her, thus giving her the wrong kind of education. Although she is tough, the young, growing Malinois is very sensitive to the attitude and moods of her handler and must be approached quietly and raised with the necessary sensitivity. Then you can raise her to be an excellent worker and companion, like the authors' own Halusetha's Be Speedy, here in 1999 during a search mission after an earthquake in Turkey.

dogs will indicate when they are tired and will slow down or even stop what they are doing. After a short rest they can pick up where they left off. As mentioned previously, even when she is tired or hot, the Malinois continues to work, going on and on, even when overworking becomes fatal. And this is another problem handlers encounter when training Malinois.

In 1998 a police force abroad asked us for help because some of their unrelated Malinois had died of exhaustion after training. At our request, they described the training in detail, and so we discovered that the dogs were asked to work out a 1.5-mile (2.5-km) track on a sunny day, after which they were to attack a flying decoy.

While the combination of activities is excellent for well-trained police dogs, it physically overtaxed the dogs-in-training.

Before the police force contacted us, we already knew that when a dog works out a half-mile (1-km) track on a sunny day, her body temperature can rise to over 104.2°F (40.1°C), and her heart and respiration rates rise too. In this case, the additional bite work at the end of the track caused hyperthermia (107.35°F/41.86°C) and complete exhaustion, which led to the dogs' deaths.

When a dog's body temperature is 106.7°F (41.5°C), she is in serious trouble. Sustaining a body temperature over 107.6°F (42°C), even for a short time, is fatal for a dog. For more information regarding this, see our books *K9 Professional Tracking* and *K9 Complete Care* (Brush Education).

In our report to the police force, we advised them to separate the tracking and bite-work sessions to avoid such physical stress on their Malinois, who, true to character, did not indicate they were tired. To protect your Malinois, you, the handler, must determine when the pauses should come in the work because your dog will not stop on her own. The positive aspect to this is that if you are careful and are giving your dog the health breaks she needs, your Malinois can work for a long time, only truly needing short pauses during the work to gather strength or cool off.

Another pro—and con—about training and working with a Malinois is her uncanny ability to "think ahead" as she works out a problem. A Malinois can invent other ways to perform certain exercises, and as a dog handler you must be prepared for this eventuality. Her ability to do this can be an advantage as well as a disadvantage. For example, in search work, if a search and rescue (SAR) Malinois can't reach her goal in a certain way, she will look for another way to meet her goal. You, the handler, need not show her the way. The downside to this is that while SAR Malinois are very independent, you must ensure they don't run the show—the handler's input is crucial to making sure area searches are thorough and complete.

Figure 4.12 While other dogs will indicate when they are tired, your Malinois will just keep going, sometimes at risk to her own life. Make sure your dog takes sufficient rest breaks during her work and play. Relaxing exercises after training and real-time missions are also recommended. (Dog Training Center, Oosterhout)

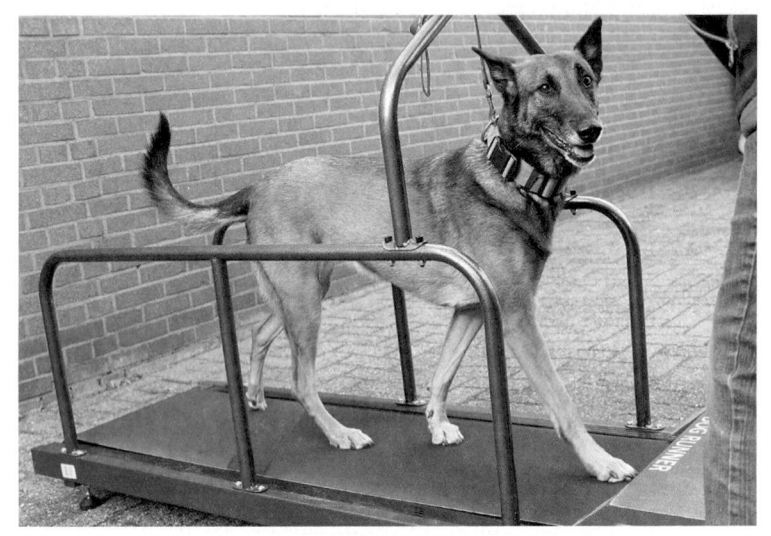

Figure 4.13 Sports dogs, service dogs, and other working dogs need a lot of training to do their jobs well. Dog treadmills help these dogs maintain top condition, even when it is too cold or hot outdoors to go for a walk. (Ruud Haak/Sabine Schümer)

Handlers often have problems with their Malinois's speed—physical and mental. First, they are surprised by their dogs' level of activity while working and then they make the mistake of asking too much from their dogs. But, when you give a Malinois too much encouragement and support, and offer her too many tasks or exercises at once, she becomes overloaded and will begin to display overactive, even neurotic, behaviors—running in circles, excessive barking, and so on. By the time her behaviors have noticeably changed, you, the handler, will be unable to contain her, and your working relationship with her will come to an end.

Unfortunately, we have encountered this bad situation too often in the last decade with K9 handlers here in Europe and elsewhere. The Malinois requires a totally different approach than most other dogs, and, as a handler, you must be aware and proactive during training.

5

The Malinois as Police Dog

In Ancient Times

Tracking dogs have served forensic investigations for thousands of years, at least as far back as 400 BCE. An ancient papyrus found in Egypt contains a satire by Sophocles (496–406 BCE) called *Ichneutai* (*The Tracking Dogs*). This somewhat risqué burlesque describes Hermes's theft of Apollo's cattle, a well-known story in Greek mythology. In the satire, satyrs, masquerading as herding dogs, pursue the track of the stolen herd and the robber. Greeks at the time of Sophocles were thus well-acquainted with the use of dogs for such tracking work.

Later, in his *Naturalis Historia*, the Roman Empire's Pliny (23–79 CE) describes six categories of dogs: *villatici* (home or guard dogs), *pastorales pecuarii* (shepherd dogs), *venatici* (hunting dogs), *pugnaces* and *bellicosi* (fighting or war dogs), *pedibus celeres* (sighthounds), and *nares sagaces* (tracker dogs).

Much later, in 1473, a book titled *Puoch von den valken, habichten, sperbern, pfaeriden, und hunden* (*Book of Hawks, Goshawks, Sparrow-hawks, Horses, and Dogs*) by Heinrich Mynsinger was published. Mynsinger bases his narrative on much older sources

Figure 5.01 "The Lead Dog on the Track" from *Livre de Chasse* (*Book of the Hunt*) written between 1387 and 1388 by Gaston III/X of Foix-Béarn, also called Gaston Phoebus (1331–1391). He was one of the greatest huntsmen of his day and hunted his entire life. He died of a stroke while washing his hands after returning from a bear hunt.

and speaks of regular police-dog training, which involved teaching dogs to stand up against a man clothed "in a stout coat of skins lest the dog should bite him during his education." The dogs were also trained to track the trail of a thief, much in the same way that bird dogs (spaniels, setters, pointers) are taught to search for partridge and quail. Mynsinger also describes how one Dr. Meurer wrote about the tracking work of dogs and their training in 1460, basing his views on English standards.

Figure 5.02 Different stages of hunting and different animals are illustrated in *Book of the Hunt*. This classic on medieval hunting has exquisite miniatures that not only illustrate the hunt but also animal behavior and health. This miniature is called "Concerning the Distemper of Dogs and Its Treatment."

Helping Town Soldiers

Police dogs have carried out their work in a variety of protection services for hundreds of years. For as long as humans have documented history, the dog has been companion and guardian to the men protecting the peace. First, he was the faithful comrade of the old-time night watchman, also called the town soldier, with his horn and his halberd, and now he takes his place in the police surveillance and intelligence services.

It is not easy to determine the precise moment the dog became the night watchman's helper. An early 17th-century woodcut illustrates a dog in this role, showing a town soldier on duty in the

Figure 5.03 This early 17th-century woodcut shows a town soldier on duty in the Belgian town of Antwerp accompanied by a dog. We see the dog at the first command, helping his master by boldly biting the legs of a villain.

Belgian town of Antwerp accompanied by a dog. The city archives mention that the first night watchman in Antwerp was chartered in 1597, and by 1627 there were 32 men on duty.

It is conceivable that dogs accompanied these men. Though simplistic in design, the woodcut's dog is similar in build to the matin and sheepdog types. The woodcut also reveals that these early police dogs were as apt to bite as they are nowadays: we see the dog helping his master by boldly biting the legs of the villain!

The weapons of the night watchmen seen in the front of the woodcut show us that they performed dangerous work. The halberd and the long saber were used to bring wrongdoers to the lockup, and in the background town soldiers can be seen doing just that. Together with these weapons, the night watchmen made increasing use of their police dogs, as can be seen in a 1786 print called *New Year's Greetings of the Night Watchmen from the Belgian Town of Leuven*, which includes a poem (author unknown) that valorizes the town soldier's task:

> Although the warriors have left the town,
> Still necessary are the town soldiers,
> Who during the night make their round,
> So everything will go well and sound.
> These are fourteen faithful men,
> During night keeping together as best they can,
> To stamp out wrongs on the street,
> And find out what's going on, indeed.

The city of Leuven (French: Louvain), the capital of the province of Flemish Brabant in Belgium, has one of the oldest-known police services to use dogs. The New Year's woodcut depicting town soldiers and their dogs and was widely distributed. However, in an ordinance from January 31, 1786, issued by the Louvain magistrate, these biting dogs are referred to with some derision: "during days and nights in the streets of this town walk different sorts of bigger dogs, like Danes, mastiffs, and sheepdogs that cause mischief, and none of such dogs may walk free in the streets of this town without muzzle under penalty of a fine of 6 guilders for each dog."

After the French Revolution in 1793, the use of police dogs in Belgium was abolished. The Human Rights Manifesto declared by the new regime in Belgium, after the French occupation, included a ban on dogs attacking people. This ban may have been

THE MALINOIS AS POLICE DOG

Figure 5.04 The city of Leuven's police service was one of the first to use dogs. This 1786 woodcut, *New Year's Greetings of the Night Watchmen from the Belgian Town of Leuven*, depicts the town soldiers and their dogs. Seven years after this woodcut was made, the use of police dogs in Belgium was abolished.

prompted by police dogs becoming too aggressive for public acceptance.

Dog Training in Malines

More than a century passes after the abolition of Belgian police dogs before any further mention is made of dogs training for tracking and protection work. Around 1890 dog enthusiasts around the Belgian city of Malines started to systematically train their short-haired Belgian shepherd dogs for protection and tracking work. Louis Huyghebaert, as you now know, encouraged the training of the Malinois.

On January 9, 1890, Louis Huyghebaert, at the insistence of Professor Reul, wrote an open letter in *Chasse et Pêche* about the poor state of the shepherd dog in Belgium, mainly a result of the decline of the large sheep flocks because of industrialization in Belgium. "There are no more than five sheepdogs worthy of the name in the hands sheep-flock owners . . . of course, with no sheep to herd, the work of driving and herding sheep will not maintain the innate character of other sheepdogs, so they must be subjected to other, more general, training exercises."

Chasse et Pêche editor-in-chief Van der Snickt wrote a comprehensive answer that he finished with: "We are all in agreement: tests for watchdogs are urgent, but how are we going to practice?"

Reul and Van der Snickt saw the dogs in Malines, especially Louis Huyghebaert's own Tom at work, and they wrote about it in the same magazine:

> We have seen the way in which Cora I (Mr. Opdebeeck) and Fram and Tom (Mr. Huyghebaert) practice in Malines.
>
> Tom stands on a pole and stays there until he is called back by a faint sound made by his unseen master, standing at a distance. Tom's hearing must be perfect to be able to perceive this noise at such a distance.
>
> In a home environment, the dog will immediately lie under the chair of his master. A stranger may touch him, but as soon as his master says "Attention," the dog makes it quite plain that no one may move to touch the dog or his master—in fact, no one may move at all.
>
> Tom leaves the cats alone, but at the slightest command he will bite their necks. On signal, he also rushes to a straw doll that is left in the field. No doubt, he would do this if he met a villain.
>
> While we walked together along the canal, Mr. Huyghebaert gave me his wallet and, while Tom was not watching, I threw the wallet in the bush, about 3 meters [10 ft] from the road. After walking on for a fair distance, Tom's master began to search his pockets and gesticulated as if he

Figure 5.05 The October 15, 1896, edition of the Belgian magazine *Sport universel illustré* included this picture and the caption: Every time we see Mr. Huyghebaert's Tom, we are impressed by his impeccable shape and every remarkable point on his head: ears of steel, slightly forward; round eyes of ebony black, sparkling with intelligence and gaining in expression in contrast with his pale color. Tom is standing on a pole and stays there until he is called back by a very light noise made by his master (situated so far away as to be invisible). His hearing must be perfect in order to be able to perceive the noise at such a distance. (*Onze Hond* Archive)

had lost something. Immediately, the dog went back to the place where we had briefly paused and came back without having found anything. Seeing his master still inspecting his pockets, he ran back quickly, first tracking and then searching with his nose in the air. Soon he came back with a triumphant look in his eyes and the wallet in his mouth.

In the *Chasses et Pêche* article, Van der Snickt also writes of the jumps and the special way the dogs could retrieve on the ground and out of the water. In conclusion, he writes:

> This proves that the shorthaired shepherds we saw at work are valuable dogs, true friends, in whose company one can spend the whole day, with whom only conversation is missing. Besides the benefits that they provide daily, one of them can save your life if you are travelling through a dangerous area and are attacked by a suspicious character. What needs to be done to make these remarkable dogs, the human's best friends, useful?
>
> 1st. Establish a breed, a family of shepherd dogs, whose pure origin is made clear by exhibitions and the studbooks of the Societé Royale St. Hubert.
>
> 2nd. Set up trials in which only purebred dogs, registered in the mentioned studbooks, will be allowed to participate.

In 1897 Van der Snickt writes in *Chasses et Pêche*:

> We went to Mr. Huyghebaert in Malines to establish a practical program because of his open letter of January 9. What we have summarized will be obligatory and free exercises.
>
> The first are:
>
> 1st. Lying down in a certain spot on command, preferably on signal.
> 2nd. Staying while his master leaves and only on command following his master.
> 3rd. Heeling.
> 4th. Guarding an object: bike, car, boat, package, etc.
> 5th. Retrieving on the ground.
> 6th. Retrieving from the water.
> 7th. Jumping over obstacles, height and width.
> 8th. Not barking.
> 9th. Waiting patiently in front of a door for as long as his master stays inside.
> 10th. Refusing food given by strangers.
> 11th. Defending his master if he is attacked.
>
> The free exercises can change endlessly.

Oddly, more than six years passed before such exercises and tests took place in Belgium. Organizing the exercises was time consuming, disagreements about the appearance and color of the dogs (as is noted earlier in this book), and ensuing battles between different clubs, held up the work needed to put the tests in place.

Dogs as Police Assistants

The idea of using dogs as police assistants was first broached by Austrian lawyer and cynologist Dr. Hans Gustav Adolf Gross, often called the father of criminal investigation. The release of his book *Handbuch für Untersuchungsrichter, Polizeibeamte, Gendarmen* (*Handbook for Magistrates, Police Officials, and Military Policemen*) in 1893, marked the birth of criminalistics. The work combined in one system fields of knowledge that had not previously been integrated—for example, psychology and science—and which could be successfully used against crime. Gross also adapted some fields to the needs of criminal investigation, such as crime-scene photography. In 1896, in the Austrian gendarmerie's yearbook, he published "A Police Assistant," a plea for the use of police dogs. In the article, he writes, "Above all, the dog should be a faithful, always alert, always attentive companion, who is equipped with far sharper senses than man, perceives much more than man, and so can warn him about the dangers of objects, as well as about many other circumstances that man would have otherwise overlooked."

In Austria it was not until 1901 that Kamillo Windt, head of the Vienna Police Detection Office, recommended the use of dogs in the security service. The security guard's central inspector opposed it, but his 1902 successor welcomed Windt's proposal. Windt also introduced dactyloscopy (fingerprint identification) to Austria after Paris's example, and after reading news about the Ghent police, had the idea to employ four-legged police helpers. A letter from the Central Inspectorate on April 5, 1902, states,

Figure 5.06 The father of criminal investigation, Dr. Hans Gustav Adolf Gross, published his plea for police dogs, "A Police Assistant," in 1896, in which he outlined the kind of dog that would help the police officer in his duties.

"the use of dogs as companions of the district offices in the undeveloped area of Vienna is under negotiation in the Central Inspectorate, and practical experience is also under way." The "practical experience" mentioned here was gained by a police officer from the Josefsdorf Station on the Kahlenberg, who in the spring of 1902 had found a dog on the street. Kuno guided his master as he conducted surveillance walks.

PoliceCed Dogs in Germany

In Hildesheim, Germany, in 1896, a few police-dog lovers launched an initiative to encourage training dogs for surveillance tasks and tracking, based on Dr. Gross's article. This was a private initiative that was only tolerated by the government, which had nothing to do with its organization. In the following years, Berlin's police chief, Robert Gerlach, was the main promoter of dog brigades in Germany.

As soon as dogs were inducted into police work, they captured the interest of journalists and the public in different countries. Interest increased significantly when they began to work as "detectives," investigating criminal cases. The value of the police dog was fully recognized when the first successes in solving homicides were recorded. From then on, police dogs were popular, both with the public and the police.

The first milestones police dogs achieved in suspect identification cannot be mentioned without also discussing Inspector Bussenius from Braunschweig in Germany. He championed the use of police dogs and was a good police-dog trainer. His work with dogs in Braunschweig did much to support the police-dog movement. In particular, his work with German shepherd Harras von der Polizei in the Duwe murder case gave the world early proof of the value of using dogs while investigating homicide cases. Harras's success in the Duwe case is often seen as a turning point in the history of the police dog.

Here's what happened: An 11-year-old girl was killed at the Hagenhof farm in the German village of Königslutter near Braunschweig on June 3, 1903. The forensic research team did not come up with any results, although one of the farmhands was a suspect. After days of continuous but fruitless investigation, the public prosecutor asked Inspector Bussenius and Harras to try to find the murderer. Soon after they arrived at the Hagenhof farm, four days after the homicide, all 12 employees of the farm were placed in a line in the yard. Harras was then brought to the crime scene, where Bussenius commanded him to sniff the bloodstains and the surrounding area. The dog immediately picked up a track.

First, he briefly scanned one of the forensic investigators who had visited the crime scene earlier. Before long, the dog left him and continued tracking. Harras then sniffed each person standing in the line, one after the other. When he reached the eighth person in the lineup, Harras hurled himself at the man, who cried out loudly in protest. The accused man was the suspected farmhand, Duwe. The test was repeated two times. Each time, the people in the lineup changed positions, but the result was always the same: Harras hurling himself furiously at Duwe without paying the slightest

Figure 5.07 Harras, the dog that identified a farmhand named Duwe as the murderer of an 11-year-old girl near Braunschweig, Germany, in 1903. The success of Harras and his handler, Inspector Bussenius, is often seen as a turning point in the history of the police dog.

Harras,
de ontdekker van den moordenaar Duwe.

attention to the other people. After that Duwe was arrested. In the beginning, Duwe tried to deny the murder, but he soon gave a full confession. Duwe was condemned to death. A dog enthusiast sent one Reichsmark to the Braunschweig police department a week after the verdict so that the police could buy the dog a reward: one beef steak.

It took only a short time before other dogs and their handlers demonstrated their ability to expose murderers. Fridolin Schmidt wrote about this phenomenon in his 1911 book, *Polizeihund-Erfolge und Neue Winke* (*Police Dog Successes and Tips*):

> In this way, rapidly one case after the other was solved, so that we can now look back upon a considerable number of murder cases successfully settled by the work of German shepherd dogs. This success cannot only be attributed to the perfect aptitude of the dogs, but certainly also to our bold dog handlers. This work has a special value, not only providing important information about the criminal cases but also information allowing authorities to assess the value of the dog in criminal investigation. These successes are also helpful in convincing the public of the value of the police dog.

In October 1909, the Verein für deutsche Schäferhunde (German Shepherd Dog Society), also called the SV, offered 25-mark rewards to dog handlers for every homicide case successfully solved by a German shepherd dog. Over a period of 18 months, the SV paid this cash prize 18 times!

THE IMPORTANCE OF THE HANDLER

These first criminal investigations by dogs caused quite a stir all over the world. The police-dog movement, at that time still in its infancy, profited substantially. But the police-dog literature of these early years includes some miraculous stories. Most of the trainers, together with the journalists writing the accounts, speak in exaggerated terms about the results achieved by the dogs. Within police and judicial circles of the period, police-dog work was fully trusted, and the clues provided by the dogs were accepted as solid evidence. Based on what we know today, however, these results were often influenced by the dogs' handlers or the "most likely" suspects. In short, the police dogs' ability in criminal investigations was highly overestimated, which led to many errors.

An event described by J. Hansmann in the first volume of *Zeitschrift für Hundeforschung* (*Journal of Dog Research*) in 1931 illustrates how an incorrect human interpretation of a police dog's work can result if the dog is not

Figure 5.08 During the early 1900s, police-dog work was fully trusted, and the clues provided by the dogs were accepted as solid evidence. However, these results were often influenced by the dogs' handlers or the "most likely" suspects, leading to many errors.

brought back to the crime scene to conduct a thorough, repeated search of the area.

> After a burglary, indistinct footprints were found near the house, in two different places about 100 meters' [328 ft] distance from each other. A police-dog handler from Berlin started with his dog at one of these spots. The dog picked up a track leading to the railway station. There it was reported that an unknown, suspiciously behaving man with a backpack, who could be described exactly, travelled from this small station on the first morning train to Berlin.
>
> But the dog handler went back to the crime scene and brought his dog to the second place where indistinct footprints were found. The dog now followed a track for 3 kilometers [1.9 mi] in another direction to a secluded house and garden. In the garden, the dog stopped at a spot which had been recently dug up. Here the greater part of the spoils was found.

This example certainly demonstrates the value of having a good police dog working in crime investigation, but it also shows us how easily we can make mistakes in interpreting the dog's work. If the dog handler had stopped after the track leading to the railway, he might have concluded that the man with the backpack had carried the stolen goods away. This would not have led to a proper conclusion to the case.

Police Dogs in Belgium

At the end of the 19th century, it was difficult for police to guard the Belgian city of Ghent: 170,000 inhabitants were spread over 6,570.5 acres (2659 ha). Watercourses and bridges dominated the cityscape, dividing and connecting all sorts of small and large islands. In addition, Ghent conducted a busy shipping schedule, with weekly connections to London, Hull, Liverpool, Newcastle, and Galveston. The ships deposited many nasty people and beachcombers in Ghent, and their loads cast an irresistible appeal to those who would like to make money quickly without too much effort. The harbor accommodation had not kept pace with the

Figure 5.09 "If you cannot give me people, please give me dogs." Ernest van Wesemael was granted his request for canine police helpers, and the results of the initial three dogs' work was so positive that soon he had 10 dogs in his kennel. Here are the first dog handlers and dogs of Ghent's police force, proudly posing in the kennel courtyard. On the far right is the concierge Police-Lieutenant De Meyer, and in the middle of the group is De Meyer's wife, who fed and cared for the dogs. (*Onze Hond* Archive/Roger De Caluwé)

fast-growing shipping industry, and the loads were often exposed on the quays.

In the autumn of 1898, Ghent's Police Chief Commissioner Ernest van Wesemael found that his night police force was no longer sufficient to provide a sufficient guarantee of safety. He calculated that he needed at least 12 men. And so, he addressed a request to city council, which denied him, for budgetary reasons. Hereupon, Van Wesemael reacted with the famous words, as recorded by the council: "If you cannot give me people, please give me dogs."

Initially, even this request was denied. But, eventually, he received permission to train three dogs for the police work "on a trial basis." The results of the experiment were so positive that 10 dogs were employed by the end of the same year.

As the Ghent police-dog force grew, Van Wesemael made it known that he did not want visitors not wearing a uniform entering the kennels. The dogs were trained to recognize and work with anyone in a police uniform. That way, a dog did not have to partner with any one police-dog handler. By training the dogs to recognize and respect police uniforms, the dogs would also never attack uniform wearers. If everyone wore a uniform in the kennel, everything was okay. But people in civilian clothes could disturb the dogs' training.

When the young dogs were inducted into the police kennel, they at first only encountered uniformed officers who entered the area to pet the dogs, feed them, and exercise them. After some time of habituation to men in uniform, a man in civilian clothes would enter the kennel daily to tease and provoke the dogs until they showed signs of aggressiveness toward anyone not wearing a uniform. Later, the dogs were taught to throw this man to the ground by wrapping their front paws around his legs and dragging him down, and then to stand on the prostrate victim and bark until the officer with whom they were working arrived. Besides this, the dogs also learned to search old houses, to track, and to chase and capture a fleeing suspect.

The results obtained by the Ghent police dogs were so good that the press could not remain indifferent. The local Flemish press gave glowing reports of the four-legged auxiliaries, and so did the Belgian French-language press, which was also read in France. Soon, a request for information about the dog program came to Ghent from the secretary of the Paris chief commissioner. By 1907 there were 14 dog brigades in France, consisting of 61 dogs.

At the same time, other towns in Belgium followed Ghent's example. The first were Sint-Gillis, Schaarbeek, and Leuven, and by 1909, 30 municipalities in Belgium had dog brigades. All dogs working in this capacity in Belgium were Belgian shepherd dogs, and most of them were of the Groenendael—the black, long-haired Belgian shepherd—and Malinois varieties.

From then on, the use of police dogs expanded and spread throughout the world. At one point, Ghent Police Chief Commissioner Ernest van Wesemael regretted that he could not keep

Figure 5.10 The local Flemish press gave glowing reports of the four-legged auxiliaries, and so did the Belgian French-language press, which was also read in France. Soon, a request for information about the dog program came to Ghent from the secretary of the Paris chief commissioner. Very soon, other police officers from around the world also sent requests for information about Ghent's successful dog brigade. (*Onze Hond* Archive/Roger De Caluwé)

up with the demands for information about the dogs. And the dogs became tired because, in addition to their night work, they gave almost-daily demonstrations of their prowess.

The high praise for the dogs expressed in numerous newspaper articles (especially English and French) caused such a demand for shepherds that any dog resembling a Groenendael or a Malinois was exported to Argentina, England, France, Germany, Russia, and the United States. Police-dog training societies soon formed in most of these countries.

Police Dogs in the United States and United Kingdom

In October 1907, General Bringham, police commissioner of New York City, sent Lieutenant George Wakefield to Ghent to study its canine operations, after which he purchased five Belgian sheepdogs. One died on the boat ride home, so Wakefield arrived home with four: one Groenendael and three Malinois. At midnight on January 27, 1908, the department's first canine unit—Patrol Squad 1, NYPD—hit the streets. A 1908 photo shows Wakefield and his dogs leading the New York Thanksgiving Day Parade—its caption explains that it was nicknamed the K9-unit.

The first New York City police-dog program was based on the Ghent program. Young dogs were trained to regard a person in a police uniform as friendly and in civilian attire as hostile. The dogs were also used in the same manner as the Ghent dogs; from 11 p.m. until 7 a.m., the dogs patrolled the Long Island residential district. The dogs would be set to run loose in the neighborhood. Upon encountering anyone other than a man in uniform, a dog would knock the stranger to the ground, stand on him, and bark until an officer arrived.

Soon other police dog units were founded in the United States. In 1907, South Orange, New Jersey, started its first team, and one year later saw Muncie, Indiana, begin a K9 unit. In 1910 the city of

THE MALINOIS AS POLICE DOG 131

Figure 5.11 In October 1907, New York Police Lieutenant George Wakefield brought four Belgian sheepdogs from Ghent to New York to become the first police dogs in New York City. This picture shows Wakefield with two of the Belgian dogs. (*Onze Hond* Archive/Roger De Caluwé)

Figure 5.12 At midnight on January 27, 1908, the department's first canine unit, called Patrol Squad 1, NYPD, hit the streets. This photo shows Wakefield and his dogs leading the New York Thanksgiving Day Parade in 1908. A footnote explains that the unit was nicknamed the "K9 unit." (*Onze Hond* Archive/Roger De Caluwé)

Glen Ridge, New Jersey, purchased two Belgian shepherds trained in New York.

The first experiment with "official" police dogs came earlier to the United Kingdom when London's Metropolitan Police Commissioner Charles Warren tested out two bloodhounds in 1888, hoping they could help catch infamous Victorian murderer Jack the Ripper. The experiment failed; one bit the commissioner and then both dogs ran off, requiring a police search to find them.

In November 1907, having heard about the successful implementation of police dogs in Belgium, Superintendent J. Dobie of the North Eastern Railway Police instructed an Inspector Dobson to set up a kennel like the Belgian one. Dobson decided to use Airedale terriers as he considered them strong, hardy, and with a keen sense of smell. The first four dogs—Jim, Vic, Mick, and Ben—began patrolling Hull Docks in 1908. The scheme was extended to the Hartlepool, Middlesbrough, and Tyne docks, all of which were policed by the North Eastern Railway Police. The dogs were trained at Hull where kennels had been erected, and they were issued coats to wear in bad weather. They were only used at night and were trained to protect the police uniform, indeed to attack anyone who was not wearing one. The dogs would even growl at their own handlers when they were not in uniform.

In February 1910, a letter arrived at the police headquarters in Glasgow's St. Andrew's Square from Lieutenant-Colonel Edwin H. Richardson, who had established a dog training school at Carnoustie, along the coast from Dundee. Up to that point, Richardson had contacted every chief constable in the United Kingdom about his school, without success. According to Alastair Dinsmor, curator of the Glasgow Police Museum, "We just happened to be the ones who were in desperate need of some solution to a problem."[9] Serious crime and violent housebreakings were increasing, and concern was rising both among Glasgow residents and in police ranks. It was clear something had to be done.

Figure 5.13 In Lieutenant-Colonel Edwin Hautenville Richardson's training program, the dog had to pursue in face of revolver fire.

Richardson had bred a type of dog especially for police service. Dubbed "The Executive," these dogs were bred mainly from Airedale terriers, with collies (for their quick minds), and retrievers (for their sense of smell).

When he contacted Glasgow, Richardson's dogs had been training with army units at the Barry Buddon military base, and would go on to serve with distinction on the front lines of World War I just a few years later.

There are few historical records of the dogs' exploits on the streets of Glasgow, but one incident made the papers when a member of The Executive bit a fellow officer in 1913. The biting incident, which saw the officer take the rest of the day off with a minor injury, was reported in the *Evening Times* of February 3, 1913. The paper confirmed that the dogs would be in use for at least three years. However, despite their success, it seems the use of the dogs was phased out, and canine recruits were ultimately absent from Scottish beats until well after World War II. "Only up to about 1913 do we have records of them," said Mr. Dinsmor. "They were phased out and there was no other use of dogs until the early 1950s."[10]

First Trial in Malines, 1903

The police-dog testing conducted in the early years of the 20th century was more like demonstrations that allowed the public to view the obedience, muscle strength, and determination of the trained shepherd dogs. The exercises differ little from those described in the 1897 plan (see page 120).

You can read about the testing in Huyghebaert's "Onze Belgische Rashonden," written in 1926:

> Nothing has been added since then; certain types of exercises have disappeared, including retrieving on the ground and from the water. These useful exercises are now sometimes performed during tracking contests, which form the second category, with open-field defense dogs. What distinguishes the first from the second category is that, in the first, the exercises displayed are always the same, conducted in a conventional environment, whereas in the second, the dog is placed in front of the "unseen," and is set up to show his ability with nose work. A demonstration of first-category exercises is good propaganda for the public and allows them to appreciate the character of dogs. A prize camp in open field, however, is not aimed at the public but rather at the fanciers who want to drive the inner qualities of their own shepherds to the front through well-thought-out tests and training.

On July 12, 1903, a large exhibition for sheepdogs was held in Malines, followed one day later by a dressage competition with swimming exercises, during which the difference between the trainers from Malines and Brussels became clear. As *Chasse et Pêche* reported in 1903:

> We saw immediately that at the first meeting between trainers of shepherd dogs, the two schools, as Reul calls them, are opposite. Malines was represented by L. Opdebeeck and his three short-haired shepherds Cora I, Frits, and Thylla; Brussels with the three Groenendaels, Joubert, Bella, and Satan, presented by Mr. Coenen, police commissioner at St. Gilles (Brussels).
>
> Here's how Professor Reul writes about it: "1st. Mr. Opdebeeck throws a stick that Cora retrieves, returns, and releases at the first sign. One would truly say that this animal does not want anyone else than her masters. 2nd. Cora is placed between four objects: a hat, a block, a stick, and a collar. When her master mentions each of these objects, Cora picks them up and carries them to the end of the training area and, when commanded, retrieves them and brings them back. We intentionally confused the order of the objects, but Cora does not mind and retrieves them correctly after being given one command." After describing all the tours and jumps in the water performed by Cora, including exercises in pairs and in groups, Reul finishes his report as follows: "Good master, good dogs! The first prize is awarded to the 'Opdebeeck family,' a model of the intimate understanding between master and dogs, an example we present to the Society of Animal Protection."
>
> The demonstration given by the Brussels school's dog was also widely applauded. Police Commissioner Coenen, wearing a long "redingote" coat and high silk hat, introduced the three impressive Groenendaels with the police officers wearing gala uniforms.
>
> The dogs first had to jump a 1.3-meter- [4-ft-] high, 3.6-meter- [12-ft-] long obstacle, and then climb a wooden climbing wall 1.9 meters [6 ft] high. It was the first time Reul and numerous members of the audience had seen this "tour de force." He writes: "This exercise is very emotional, and Joubert repeated it several times in succession, to the

enthusiastic applause of the spectators." Then we saw the "work" performed by Satan and the other Groenendaels of the St. Gillian Police Service: guarding an object, attacking a villain, and so on. Professor Reul writes: "Satan has been able to show his knowledge and skills in Mechelen. The special police work of that dog is not comparable to any evidence of good training, agility, and ingenuity provided by Cora, but Satan deservedly also earned a first prize. Without difficulty, the committee obtained permission to award two first prizes of the same value. One was for Cora and the other for Satan (a special award for him)."

Police Commissioner Coenen did not take Reul's judgment well because, in his opinion, Satan showed a much better work than Cora. After writing in his magazine *Chasse et Elevage* that summer about how nice and good his police dogs were, he compared them

Figure 5.14 Mr. L. Opdebeeck and his dog Cora I, about whom Reul wrote after the dressage competition in 1903: "Good master, good dogs! The first prize is awarded to the 'Opdebeeck family,' a model of the intimate understanding between master and dogs, an example we present to the Society of Animal Protection." (*Onze Hond* Archive)

with Cora and suggested her shows of obedience, cleverness, and litheness were "circus tricks."

The commissioner was immediately put in his place by Reul: "We believe the methods of training should aim to extend the inner gifts and at the same time, through exercise, develop the most important organs, like the lungs, heart, and limbs. In this respect, I fully agree with my friend, Huyghebaert. I really could not say if his view convinced me, or my impressions persuaded him. What I can confirm, however, is that we spoke of this subject more than once, and together we decided that it is useless to sacrifice the inner traits of these dogs to make them appear more elegant." The heart of the controversy was whether training should follow the example set by Malines, which emphasized nose work and problem solving by the dog itself, without help from the handler, or the example set by Brussels, which stressed physical strength and agility, training tricks such as jumping over extremely high hurdles.

After this, the two schools took separate paths. The people from Malines went on into perfecting the training of their dogs, while others, especially from Antwerp and Brussels, were satisfied with the sloppy training of their dogs (with a focus on learned tricks rather than bringing out the natural abilities of the dogs) and in demonstrations showed exceptional achievements like huge height jumps. Certain Brussels trainers, including Mr. Moucheron, the owner of the Dax kennel, who played a leading role in this separation, took all the financial benefits of the demonstrations, for which sometimes more than 2500 entry tickets were sold, without worrying about the very unfavorable reviews of the foreign and local media. The Brussels Club du Chien Pratique, under the direction of Mr. Embrechts, made a specialty of such "shows." The good reputation of Belgian shepherds was damaged by the practice of these "professionals." And so, between 1903 and 1913, little progress was made, especially in nose work, which was not included in the "demonstrations."

Figure 5.15 Professional dog trainer Edmond Moucheron (right) held many demonstrations with his Groenendaels, bred in his kennel. Pictured here are his dogs: Dax (named after his favorite dog), Bobby Dog, Murke, Miss-Pratique, and Nick. (*Onze Hond* Archive)

Figure 5.16 Certain Brussels trainers, including Edmond Moucheron, earned a lot of money through the dog demonstrations they conducted all over the Belgian countryside and abroad. (*Onze Hond* Archive)

THE MALINOIS AS POLICE DOG 139

Foto) Oefeningen met politiehonden *(Schouten op het terrein Zorgvliet. — Onze foto brengt in beeld den hoogsten sprong (3 M. 10 c.M.), door den Belgischen politiehond Bobby Dog.*

Figure 5.17 The many demonstrations brought lots of very unfavorable reviews in the Begian and foreign professional dog press, which depicted the shows as no more than a series of circus tricks. Here is Bobby Dog of the Dax kennel, jumping a 10-foot (3.1-m) fence. (*Onze Hond* Archive)

After World War I

The boom of the Belgian police dogs became lost at the outbreak of World War I. The occupying forces confiscated the police dogs and made them serve as brave front soldiers, while the most beautiful specimens became pets for the officers.

After the end of World War I (1918), restarting the police-dog brigades was difficult. The corps leadership had to solve a lot of problems, and interest in police dogs had already come to a halt. The night police, as it once was, was abolished. Nevertheless, some dogs were still in service. Eventually, when the motorization of the police demanded the full attention of the leadership, the dog brigades in Ghent and other Belgian cities were dissolved and were not started up again for a long time.

But after those bad war years, Belgian dog fanciers did begin training police dogs again as a hobby, and so dog training gradually became a sport again. Every Belgian municipality of any significance had at least one dog-training club during the interwar period, and no weekend passed without a tournament or event being held somewhere. These events were great propaganda for the dogs. The public interest in sport training was high, which in turn fueled interest in working dog breeds and working dog breeding.

Unlike before the war, when only the Belgian shepherds sporting the accepted coats and colors (black and pale long-haired, ash-gray and pale yellow wire-haired, and pale-yellow short-haired) could participate in tournaments, after the war, shepherds of all colors and coats could participate.

The general practice of dog training for breeding continued and ensured that breeders' attention was based on the preservation and improvement of character traits in the breed. In contrast, unilateral exhibition breeding inevitably results in neglect and deterioration of working character traits.

However, the practical results of what would now be called "hobby training" do not translate into the skills service dogs need. During the interwar years, hobby training developed into a sport whose competition programs, and not the requirements for a useful service dog, inform the training exercises. This contrasts with police-dog training, after which the dog must engage in practical work in different areas and under constantly changing circumstances.

Unlike sport training programs, the KNPV, founded 1907 in the Netherlands, seeks practical end results. Thus, its selection

Figure 5.18 In post–World War II Netherlands, as after World War I, it was too expensive for most people to register their pedigreed working-dog puppies in the Dutch Dog Studbook (NHSB). At that point in the nation's history, as well, the dog's working qualities were again found to be more important than a piece of paper that did not improve the quality of the dog. And so emerged a split between pedigreed dogs and crossbred dogs. Lack of money in postwar Netherlands also showed in the quality of protective gear worn by decoys, as this picture of a worn-out bite suit from the early 1960s shows. (*Onze Hond* Archive)

program shows a significant difference from the usual competition programs in Belgium.

A POLICE DOG EVENT IN 1922

In the September 23, 1922, issue of *De Nederlandsche Hondensport* (*The Dutch Dog Sports*) is a report of a special police-dog match in Antwerp. The exercises in that match were much more practical than was usual in dog training and tournaments of that time, and there was also a tracking exercise.

> The Antwerpse Hondenliefhebbers Vereniging (Antwerp Dog Fanciers' Association) organized a contest for police dogs on September 2–3, 1922, which favored the program that is usually followed in Belgium.... There were 15 participants. As you will see in the following program, everything was quite complicated and included combinations of exercises that, while they can occur in practice, are ones the dog must work out on the spot.
>
> 1. *Tracking.* From a bloody object, the dog will follow a track, over water (over which the track layer has walked on a plank, after which the plank was removed); at the end of the track there are three cabins, each

containing a person; one of those people is the track layer, who must be identified, barked at, and guarded until the handler's arrival.

Only four dogs worked well; some did not go over the water, while others lost the track or walked back. Most dogs had no idea what tracking was.

2. *Lay down, 1.5 minutes.* This was done by only eight of the 15 dogs.

3. *Searching for a lost object.* The handler lets the dog smell an object and then sends him forward and drops the object in a place where two other similar objects are lying. Then he follows his dog and after 100 meters [328 ft] he sends the dog back to retrieve the correct object.

This very difficult exercise requires a lot of knowledge when it comes to detecting an object from similar ones, and it was even more difficult as the handler received the item only at the start of the exercise, so the item carried little of the handler's odor. This exercise was far too difficult for the dogs, who were not used to doing any real search work or tracking. Some dogs succeeded. Was it luck?

4. *Guarding an object* (bicycle, basket, coat, etc. by lottery).

5. *Attack on a stationary man who is ready to shoot with a gun.* When the dog comes within 10 meters [33 ft] of the man, he shoots in the direction of the ground and stays in the same position.

Four dogs did the job well; others did not go to the man or did not attack him.

6. *Defense of the handler.* While he walks in the direction of two fighting men, the handler is attacked by a third person; the defense must be done without a command.

Half the dogs (seven) did well; others flew to the combatants and left the handler alone, while others defended badly.

7. *Attack with obstacles.* A thief challenges the dog from far away at the top of a fence and then shoots.

The dogs had to reach him, first going around water, then over a hedge and a fence 2 meters [7 ft] high; however, the space the dogs had to navigate to reach the last obstacle was insufficient, so most dogs passed the fence; others returned to the start as soon as they could no longer see the thief's face.

8. *Water work.* Retrieving a floating man and a basket, which is placed in the water while the dog is retrieving the man. Most dogs did well.

On the whole, we can praise the attempt to practice and demand search and tracking work. Most of the leading dogs were Malinois. The winner was Killer (LOSH 14912), the Malinois male of Mr. P. Gielens, who scored 178 of the 200 points. And further, Snap (LOSH 10050), the Malinois dog of Mr. H. Hanssen, with 130 points; Rita de la Campine, the Malinois bitch of Mr. Bogemans, also with 130 points; Duc du Rupel, the Malinois dog of Mr. Vonkanel, with 127 points; and Jaks, the Groenendael of Mr. Kenis, with 117 points.

Police Dogs in the Netherlands

By 1900 the chief police commissioner of Amsterdam was in contact with his Belgian colleagues about the Belgian police-dog program. One year later, a member of the city council of Amsterdam asked to receive information from Police Chief Commissioner Ernest van Wesemael of Ghent, and representatives of the police and other city administrations also asked for information from Ghent. But they only received written information. Requests for tours and training for dog handlers were consistently refused. Van Wesemael defended his resolute refusals, saying his dogs worked at night and would be too tired out if they had to perform demonstrations during the day. Others pointed out that Van Wesemael wanted to keep the Dutch in the dark because he was an old soldier and during that period, the Belgian army did not deal with the Dutch army and police.

But dog training, especially police dog training, was already being done in the Netherlands at the beginning of the 20th century. However, the Dutch had no association to organize this training and the needed tests for these dogs, not to mention trainer instruction. In 1907, Mr. Couwenberg with his boxer Max, Mr. Van Oosten with his shepherd Hector, Mr. Steijns with his Dutch shepherd Frits, and Mr. Lokerse with his French shepherd Piet participated in the first competition for police dogs of the kennel club in Breda, where these men achieved good results with their dogs. They decided there to establish an association for police dogs in the Netherlands.

Mr. Muller, a German police officer and the judge of the German Polizeihund Verein (Police Dog Club) invited Mr. Herfkens from The Hague police to attend a September 1907 match in Hagen, Germany. There Herfkens met Mr. Kessler, who also came from The Hague.

Herfkens, Kessler, and Steijns began setting up a police-dog association in the Netherlands, like the ones in Belgium and Germany. On October 25, 1907, one month after the match in Hagen, these three men came together at the Unicorn, Steijns's drugstore in Roosendaal, and founded the Dutch Police Dogs Association, the Nederlandse Politiehonden Vereniging (NPV). The "K" in KNPV, which stands for *Koninklijke* (Royal), was added to the name later, on February 28, 1912.

The KNPV began issuing certifications in 1959, with its Police Dog 1 (PH-1) certificate, followed by Police Dog 2 (PH-2), and in 1978, Object Guarding. At the beginning of the 21st century, KNPV was also certifying dogs in Search Dog (tracking, scent-identification lineups, and search and rescue) training.

PH-1 is the standard certificate for the modern police dog. PH-2 is a certificate issued to advanced police dogs, specifically those at the top of their class. Dogs participating in a PH test should be at least two years old and must have a minimum shoulder height of about 22 inches (55 cm). Dogs should preferably not exceed a shoulder height of 28 inches (70 cm). The dogs must have good teeth and a good coat, and they must generally meet the requirements for a healthy, burly, adult dog.

Dogs belonging to one of the following varieties may be certified: sheepdog (all varieties), Doberman, giant schnauzer, Bouvier des Flandres, Airedale terrier, Rottweiler, boxer, and all crosses between these breeds. Pitbull terriers and their crosses are excluded

Figure 5.19 Today, many KNPV trained dogs are crossbred. This does not necessarily mean that these dogs' backgrounds are unknown. In fact, most breeders know the backgrounds of crossbred dogs, many of whom descend from well-known, old working lines. (*Onze Hond* Archive)

Figure 5.20 The Police Dog I (PH-1) certificate is the standard certificate for the modern police dog. The Police Dog II (PH-2) certificate is issued to the advanced police dogs, those at the top of their class. The certification tests are split into three parts, each including a variety of exercises. The first part tests basic obedience and control. Here, Othar Perle de Tourbière, owned by Mr. Jan Tinnemans, completes the Jump Over a Ditch exercise during the Dutch KNPV PH-2 Championship in 2002. (*Onze Hond* Archive)

from tests, as are dogs with docked ears and/or tails. Dogs that suffer from any disease or are visibly pregnant are not admitted to the tests, either. Also, if handlers cannot vouch for the reliability of their dogs, they may not participate in the tests.

KNPV PH-1 TEST

The certification test for PH-1 consists of three parts. Part 1 covers common skills, such as the dog's basic obedience and control. Part 2 covers specific skills for water work. Part 3 tests protection exercises. Besides these parts, there are two parts related to "general outlook": one for the dog (general obedience) and one for the handler (the way the handler presents the dog at the test). Following are the components of the test.

PART 1
A. Heeling on leash: 5 points
B. Heeling without a leash, on the right and left side of the handler: 5 points
C. Heeling next to a bicycle: 5 points
D. Down stay: 5 points
E. Refusal of offered and thrown food: 5 points
F. Refusal of found food: 5 points
G. Be silent: 5 points
H. Free jump over a 3-foot (1-m) -high hedge: 5 points
I. Jump over a 5.7-foot (1.75-m) -high wall: 5 points
J. Jump over a 10-foot (3-m) -long, 7.4-foot (2.25-m) -wide, and 3-foot (1-m) -deep ditch: 5 points
K. Searching for and retrieving small articles: 15 points

PART 2
A. Swimming across a 49-foot (15-m) -wide canal: 10 points
B. Retrieving a large object out of the water: 10 points

PART 3
A. Guarding an article: 10 points
B. Searching for a large object hidden in the woods: 25 points
C. Searching for a person hidden in the woods: 25 points
D. Transport of an arrested man: 15 points
E. Apprehending a suspect who defends himself with a stick: 35 points

Figure 5.21 Part 2 of the PH tests covers water work. Here, Mr. J. Boele's Arras retrieves a large object out of the water at the Dutch KNPV Championship in 1994. (*Onze Hond* Archive)

Figure 5.22 Part 3 of the PH tests consists of protection exercises: the most spectacular part of police-dog work that always attracts an audience, as shown here at the Dutch KNPV Championship in 2010. (*Onze Hond* Archive)

Figure 5.23 A typical Dutch exercise in Part 3 of the KNPV Police Dog certificate is Apprehending a Suspect Who Flees on a Bicycle, followed by Apprehending a Fleeing Suspect. When these exercises were first developed, the dog was allowed to bite the decoy on his back, but today (for safety reasons) the dog may only bite the decoy on the leg, as is shown here during the 2009 Dutch KNPV Championship. (*Onze Hond* Archive)

F. Refusing to obey commands given by a suspect: 20 points

G. Transport followed by apprehending a fleeing suspect: 30 points

H. Apprehending a suspect who flees on a bicycle: 30 points

I. Apprehending a fleeing suspect: 20 points

J. Apprehending a suspect who shoots with a gun: 35 points

K. Refusing to retreat from the suspect when he throws objects at the dog: 20 points

L. Transport followed by defending the handler: 30 points

M. Recall of the pursuing dog: 15 points

N. Apprehending a fleeing person who surrenders in time, followed by a transport: 20 points

POINTS TOTAL
Part 1: 65 points
Part 2: 20 points
Part 3: 330 points
General obedience: 10 points
Way of presenting: 10 points
Maximum score: 435 points

The dog must score at least 348 points to receive his certificate, and he must score at least the following number of points in the following parts of the test:

Part 1: 40 points
Part 3: Exercises B and C, 24 points
Part 3: Exercise E, 18 points
Part 3: Exercise H, 15 points
Part 3: Exercise J, 18 points

To receive a certificate *met lof* (with honors), the dog must score a total of at least 392 points and all attack exercises must be excellent.[11]

Service Dog Number 1

In the last decades many trainers and professional dog handlers have stopped working with the German shepherd dog in favor of the Malinois. This because of the poor breeding of the German shepherd dog as a working dog and a serviceable police dog. The German shepherd not only has partly hereditary physical problems, but the breed's mental condition is not what it once was.

Not everyone is happy with this switch to the Malinois. A policeman in Vienna, Austria, who works as a K9 handler and patrols with his German shepherd during the summertime in a recreation area near the Danube River told us, "I could not think

Figure 5.24 For almost a century, the German shepherd was the number one working and service dog in police, customs, and border-guard outfits, but because of a careless breeding program, by the end of the 20th century, the Malinois had taken over the role of most popular and effective working dog. Even in Germany, many police and border guards have switched to the Malinois.

about patrolling with a Malinois in this park. I wouldn't be able to look at the people—I'd have to pay so much attention to my dog and I'd have to walk much faster!" He is a rather heavy man and a very easy-going type, so for him the Malinois is much too lively!

Of course, there are still German shepherds with very good working ability, but their quantity is greatly decreasing. However, even in Germany, where everyone feels affection toward "their shepherd dog," in one decade the number of German shepherd dogs used by border police and customs officials decreased by 70 per cent. So today, in Germany, just like everywhere in the world, we see the Malinois as the number one service dog.

THE MALINOIS AS POLICE DOG 151

Figure 5.25 A witness reported a house burglary to the Dutch Police. Police officers saw that the house had been broken into but could not find the burglar. A police dog had more success. Near the ditch that adjoined the house's backyard, the police dog scented a track. The dog walked up the thin ice on the edge of the ditch, then dropped through the ice and swam right under a platform. The dog handler heard someone screaming and called his dog, who then surfaced with a very cooled-off suspect. (*Onze Hond* Archive)

Figure 5.26 The patrol dog, working with the Belgian Police, is a polyvalent police dog deployed in the context of community-oriented police care. Belgian police dogs patrol and maintain public order during football matches and other public events. (Belgian Federal Police, www.polfed-fedpol.be)

Figure 5.27 The Belgian Federal Police has about 100 specialized dog teams. Half of these are employed by the Directie hondensteun (Dog Support Board), and the other teams are active in other federal police services, including the Special Units. Each dog team (dog and handler) trained by the Dog Support Board can specialize in one discipline. The attack dog, which works in the Special Units, is considered a weapon and is used to neutralize dangerous people. (Belgian Federal Police, www.polfed-fedpol.be)

6

The Malinois in Other Roles

Herding Trials

Besides as a police and military dog, the Malinois works in a lot of other areas, such as one of her original jobs: herding. Owners of herding breeds use a standardized test to measure a dog's instincts and trainability for herding. The initial test is an instinct test for which the dog needs no training. The judge is looking for the dog's ability to move and control livestock by fetching or driving. The purpose of the competitive herding trial program is to preserve and develop the herding skills inherent in the herding breeds, and to demonstrate that they can perform the useful functions for which they were originally bred. Malinois exhibiting basic herding instincts can be trained to compete in herding trials.

In these trials, dogs work in two different styles related to the landscapes where the shepherds and flocks originally lived and worked. In the Collecting Style, the sheep often stand in widely spread, hilly fields. If you want to move sheep in such an environment, you need a dog to collect the sheep and bring them to the farmer, who stands at the entrance of the field and uses whistle signals to send the dog out to collect the sheep. The dog can

Figure 6.01 According to a legend circulating in the Magdeburg, Germany, region, the shepherd Thomas Koppehele, who lived around 1240, is said to have found a golden treasure while herding sheep. He donated the treasure to the Archbishop of Magdeburg who, according to the legend, was thus able to significantly advance the construction of the Magdeburg Cathedral. Out of gratitude, the archbishop installed a stone image of the shepherd and his servant with the dogs just above the north entrance of the cathedral, where it is still visible today. (*Onze Hond* Archive)

Figure 6.02 Here, on the beautiful heathlands of the Veluwe in 1930, Dutch shepherd Willem Mouw's dogs were happy to see the photographer and writer visiting them. Well, one of them—the other one was doing his job. Willem always had enough time for a chat. (*Onze Hond* Archive)

Figure 6.03 On another visit to the heath, this time in 1941, Willem Mouw talked with his visitor about a dog he used to have, called Fik, his favorite: "He was a rascal! He did not bite the sheep, but he squeezed them with his jaws if they walked away." While talking, Willem let his thirsty dog drink out of his wooden shoe. (*Onze Hond* Archive)

hear the whistle blasts over a long distance. She works behind the sheep and drives them to the farmer. The head of the flock of sheep is wide because the dog runs behind the flock, driving the sheep forward. In the Collecting Style we see especially the border collie and Australian kelpie; these breeds are strictly collecting or driving herders and so are excluded from the trials in the Traditional Style.

In the Traditional Style, the shepherd uses dogs as walking fences to move the herd to a place to graze, often adjacent to fields that are sown or planted. The style is employed also by the shepherd who uses the dog to keep the sheep out of areas that should not be grazed. Therefore, these dogs are often found alongside the moving flock, running back and forth between the head of the flock and the tail. In this style, the herded flock is like

Figure 6.04 In the Traditional Style herding test, the shepherd uses the dogs as walking fences to move the herd to a place to graze, often adjacent to fields that are sown. The shepherd also uses this style to keep the sheep out of the areas that should not be grazed. These dogs are often found on the sides of a moving flock, running from the head of the flock to the tail and back again. (*Onze Hond* Archive)

a long ribbon of sheep. In pasture areas, the dog mostly runs along natural boundaries like cart tracks, different crops, tree edges, or ditches, to keep the sheep within their grazing area. At the end of the day, the shepherd and dog take the flock back home, through the village. The Traditional Style is practiced by Belgian, German, and Dutch sheepdogs.

The Herding Working Test (HWT) is the entry-level Traditional Style test. The dog and handler take on a short course in which the dog must use both her learned abilities and instincts to do the work. The dog takes sheep out of a corral and then along a track designated by the judges. She must first make a stop and then angle the flock into the pasture. The sheep are to graze here, but when the judge gives a signal, the dog must gather the flock again and take them back into the corral.

The next stage in the Traditional Style tests is International Herding Trial 1 (IHT-1). The test is the same, but the degree of difficulty goes up—what a judge might overlook in HWT is now penalized with docked points. From IHT-1, dog and handler move on to IHT-2, where the test is different, and much more difficult. For instance, the dog must herd the sheep over a bridge that spans no water in the middle of a field. This is hard work, because while a bridge spanning water would be a natural path for sheep, a bridge you can walk beside is not—sheep would rather not take the bridge if they can simply walk on the ground. The IHT-3 test is the highest level of Traditional Style test and includes other, difficult exercises: bridge over land, as well as a funnel, through which only one sheep can pass at a time. IHT-3 also may test the dog's ability to keep the flock at the side of the path when a vehicle approaches, and in other difficult situations.

Detection Work

Although herding was the first task the Malinois undertook for humans, today she works in many areas: search and rescue (SAR) and detection work (e.g., agricultural items, blood traces, bomb-making component traces, cadavers, currency, drugs, explosives, firearms, and tobacco). During the daily routine, detection dog handlers and their canines may search cargo shipments, luggage, and passenger carry-on bags. They are most frequently employed at airports, border crossings, and ports. Handlers must be familiar with each behavioral signal their dogs display, and they are responsible for initiating a search if their dogs signal they have found contraband.

To support the SAR and detection dog's work, in 2007 the KNPV introduced a new program for scent work in tracking, scent discrimination, and SAR work in area and rubble searches. This new program had two primary motivations: first, scent work was becoming increasingly more important in real-world police applications; and second, the program could be a way to bring new, younger people into the KNPV family to reverse the loss of membership in recent years. All participating handlers in the new program had to be working with KNPV Basic Certificate search dogs.

Figure 6.05 In 2007 the KNPV introduced a new program for scent work in tracking, scent discrimination, and SAR work. All candidates for these new certificates first must secure their KNPV Basic Certificates. In this 2002 photo, Othar Perle de Tourbière, owned by Mr. Jan Tinnemans, is ready for nosework. (*Hondensport & Sporthonden*/Theo Dijkman)

KNPV BASIC CERTIFICATE SEARCH DOGS

The purpose of the Basic Certificate in searching is to assess the dog's skills and prepare her for the next certificates: Tracking Dog A and B, Scent Discrimination A and B, Rubble Search A and B, and Area Search A and B. The dog and handler team participating in these examinations must have completed the Basic Certificate first.

In the Basic Certificate, a judge assigns a grade of at least 0 points and no more than 5 points for each of the exercises and components, except for the exercises and components for which a higher rating is mentioned (see the exercises in Part 3, below). Only whole points are awarded. The rating of the points is:

5 = excellent
4 = good
3 = sufficient
2 = insufficient
1 = bad
0 = very bad or not completed

PART 1
A. Heeling on leash with tempo changes: 5 points
B. Heeling without a leash, at the right and left side, with noise distractions: 5 points

Coping with distractions: 5 points
C. Heeling without a leash through a moving group of talking people: 5 points
    Coping with distractions: 5 points
D. Down stay during another dog's performance: 5 points
E. Leaving the dog alone and picking up later: 5 points
F. Sending out: 5 points
    Followed by calling the dog: 5 points
G. Carrying and handing over the dog: 5 points

Total Part 1: 50 points

PART 2
A. Free jumping over an obstacle 1 meter (3.3 ft) high: 5 points
B. Jumping over a 1.5-meter (5-ft) -wide ditch: 5 points
C. Walking on an open staircase (10–12 steps): 5 points
D. Walking a plank 0.5 meters (1.6 ft) wide and 5 meters (16.4 ft) tall, about 2 meters (6.7 ft) off the ground: 5 points
E. Crawling through a straight tunnel with a diameter of 0.5 meters (1.6 ft) and a length of 5 meters (16.4 ft), the end of which is not visible: 5 points
F. Walking over unpleasant materials, stopping once: 5 points
G. Refusing found food: 5 points
H. Searching and indicating or retrieving three objects carrying human scent that are 3–5 centimeters (1.2–2 in) long and 1–3 centimeters (0.4–1.2 in) wide: 3 × 5 points (15 points)

Total Part 2: 50 points

PART 3
A. Searching and indicating two objects carrying human scent: first, a weapon (gun), second, a 50-centimeter (19.7-in) -long crowbar. The dog must systematically

search for and indicate these objects. The search area is about 100 meters (328 ft) long and at least 15 meters (49 ft) wide, and is set up in many different places (e.g., in a forest, on the shore, along a ditch, beside a parking lot). The dog may search for up to seven minutes.

Way of searching: 10 points; way of indicating: 10 points = 20 points

B. Finding and locating a sitting or prone person on a partially covered and partially open area of approximately 70 × 70 meters (230 × 230 ft). The dog must search for and independently indicate the hidden person by barking, bringsel alert, or by recall. (See our description of these alerts in "Area Search," later in this chapter.) The dog may search for up to seven minutes.

Behavior of the handler: 10 points; way of searching: 10 points; way of indicating: 10 points = 30 points

C. Working out a track that is about 200 steps (about 150 m, or 492 ft) long, on a lawn or meadow. The track layer should walk slowly and change direction twice. On the track is one object (e.g., a knife, screwdriver, gun, bunch of keys), and the end of the track is marked by another object: a gun. Both objects carry the track layer's scent. The dog may search for up to seven minutes.

Way of working out the track: 15 points; way of indicating the two objects: 10 points = 25 points

D. Scent discrimination of an object on a sorting board. The dog must sort out and retrieve a 2 × 2 × 10–centimeter (0.8 × 0.8 × 3.9–in) stainless steel tube with a wall thickness of 0.1–0.2 centimeters (0.04–0.07 in), which someone has held for three minutes and laid on a sorting board with two other identical tubes that are not scented. The dog may search for up to three minutes.

Method of scent discrimination: 15 points; way of retrieving: 5 points = 20 points

Total Part 3: 95 points

General obedience and presentation is assessed throughout the exam and are assigned a value of up to 10 points each.

Points Total:
Part 1: 50 points
Part 2: 50 points
Part 3: 95 points
General obedience: 10 points
Presentation: 10 points
Maximum score: 215 points

The dog must receive at least 172 points to receive her Basic Certificate Search Dogs, and she must receive at least the following number of points in these parts of the test:

In Part 1: 35 points
In Part 2: 35 points
In Part 3: 65 points

To receive a Basic Certificate Search Dogs *met lof* (with honors), the dog must receive at least 193 points.

After receiving this certificate, the dog can do exams for the other KNPV certificates: Tracking Dog A and B, Scent Discrimination A and B, Rubble Search A and B, and Area Search A and B.

Figure 6.06 One of the exercises dogs must successfully master for their KNPV Basic Certificate is scent discrimination of an object on a sorting board. The dog must sort out and retrieve a stainless-steel tube that a specific person has held in hand for three minutes. The tube lies with two other equal but neutrally scented tubes on the sorting board. (Dog Training Center, Oosterhout)

Figure 6.07 Here, Igor Perle de Tourbière (Mr. Jo Slangen) tracks at the 2003 FMBB World Championship for Belgian Shepherds, at which he took third place. (*Hondensport & Sporthonden*/Theo Dijkman)

TRACKING DOG A

To gain this certificate, the dog must work out a two-hour-old track that is about 1000 steps (700 m, or 2296.6 ft) long and was laid by a track layer who walked along an open terrain, consisting of grassland or arable land. The track layer should change direction eight times and place three objects carrying only his or her odor on the track—perhaps a knife, a screwdriver, a gun, a bunch of keys, a wallet, or a pair of tongs. At the end of the track, the track layer will place a larger object, such as a gun, a cash box, a garment, or a bag of tools. The dog may search for up to 30 minutes. The exercise starts with a signal from the judge and ends when the dog has barked or otherwise indicated the final object.

Way of working out the track: 45 points
Indicating four objects: 4 × 5 points = 20 points
General obedience: 10 points
Presentation: 10 points
Maximum score: 85 points

The dog must score at least 68 points to get the Tracking Dog A Certificate, and to receive a certificate *met lof* (with honors), the dog must score a total of 76 points.

TRACKING DOG B

For the level-B tracking test, the dog must figure out a three-hour-old track that is about 2000 steps (1400 m, or 4593 ft) long. The track, again, is laid by a slow-walking track layer through open terrain (grassland or arable land) or another terrain with little vegetation. Crossing paved and unpaved roads should not present a problem to the dog working on this track. The track layer should change direction 10 times, and the shapes of the turns must include an acute angle (45°) and an obtuse angle (135°). Another of the turns must trace out a half-circle with a cross section of at least 30 meters (98 ft). All the other turns should be executed at right angles (90°). Four objects that smell of the track layer should be left on the track, as is one similarly scented object at the track's end. Finally, half an hour before the dog is allowed to work out the track, a distraction track is laid by another track layer, which crosses over two legs of the original track. The distraction track may not cross the first and last leg of the track. The dog is given up to 45 minutes to search.

Way of working out the track: 55 points
Indicating five objects: 5 × 5 points = 25 points
General obedience: 10 points
Presentation: 10 points
Maximum score: 100 points

Figure 6.08 In Tracking Dog B, the dog must figure out a three-hour-old track that is about 2000 steps (1400 m, or 4593 ft) long. (*Hondensport & Sporthonden*/Theo Dijkman)

The dog must score at least 80 points to get the Tracking Dog B certificate, and to receive a certificate *met lof* (with honors), she must score at least 90 points in total.[12]

SCENT DISCRIMINATION A

In this test, dogs are offered the odor of a person and then must find the matching odor in a lineup of possibilities. The dog must select the tube that carries this specific odor instead of the four other tubes that appear identical but carry the odors of four other people. The allowed time for each sorting test, including giving the odor, is three minutes.

The test is administered using 20 identical, stainless-steel, square tubes, 2 × 2 × 10 centimeters (0.8 × 0.8 × 3.9 in), with wall thickness ranging from 0.1 to 0.2 centimeters (0.04–0.08 in). These tubes must have a neutral scent—so no odor other than that of the material of which they are made. To give the tubes odor, five people are given four neutral tubes each, between one and 24 hours before the sorting test. They must hold the tubes in their hand for five minutes. Then, the tubes are stored in glass jars. The judge designates one person to be the "suspect." Track layers are not allowed to participate as odor donors in a sorting test as their familiar scents could distract participating dogs.

One of the suspect's tubes and one tube from each of the four other people are placed in a row on the sorting board. About

Figure 6.09 The Scent Discrimination exercise is a "match to sample" process. Dogs are given a sample odor and must find the matching odor among several alternatives. For Scent Discrimination A, the dog must retrieve a tube that carries the odor of a specific person, instead of any one of the other four otherwise-identical tubes that each carry the odor of a different person. This photo shows the construction of the tube clamp on the KNPV sorting board. (Dog Training Center, Oosterhout)

3 meters (10 ft) away from the end of the sorting board, the judge gives the handler a jar containing a tube with the suspect's odor. The handler offers the tube to the dog to smell, and then sends her over to the sorting board to find the matching odor and bring it back to the handler.

The dog must do the sorting test three times with other scented tubes to investigate and the correct tube always placed in different places in the lineup. Before each sorting test, the handler gives the dog the scent. For each sorting test, the dog can score up to 15 points for sorting out and up to 5 points for retrieving.

Way of sorting out: 3 × 15 points = 45 points
Way of retrieving: 3 × 5 points = 15 points
General obedience: 10 points
Presentation: 10 points
Maximum score: 80 points

The dog must score at least 64 points to get the Scent Discrimination A Certificate, and to receive a certificate *met lof* (with honors), she must score a total of at least 72 points.

SCENT DISCRIMINATION B
To gain the second scent discrimination certificate, the dog must work out two sorting boards, each with seven tubes, including the scent of a control person and that of the designated suspect. The dog must first find and retrieve the tube of the control person from each board. After successfully doing this, the dog must find and retrieve the suspect's tube from each board. For each of the four sorting tests, from the moment she is given the scent of the control person, the dog is allowed three minutes to work it all out.

Five people are given two neutral tubes at least one hour and up to 24 hours before the start of the sorting test. They must hold the tubes for five minutes. In addition to these five, the control person and the suspect are given three neutral tubes that they must hold

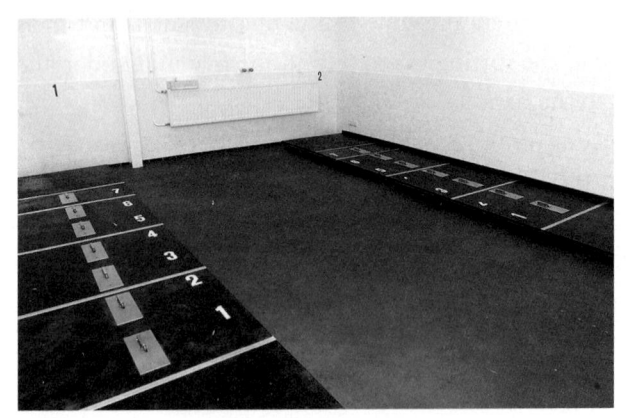

Figure 6.10 In Scent Discrimination B, there are two sorting boards, each with seven tubes, including one containing the scent of a control person and one with the scent of a designated person who acts as a suspect. The control person's tube, the suspect's tube, and those of five other people are placed in a row on the sorting board. Here is a professional sorting platform owned by the Dutch Police. (Ruud Haak/KLPD)

Figure 6.11 In Scent Discrimination B, the dog first finds and retrieves the control person's tube from each board. If she is successful, she then must find and retrieve the suspect's tube from each board. The exercise ends after the dog has correctly sorted the tubes four times. (Ruud Haak/KLPD)

for five minutes. When the tubes are ready, they are stored in glass jars marked as follows: A for the control person, X for the suspect, and B to F for the others.

One control tube, one suspect tube, and one of each of the five others are placed in a row on the sorting board. To determine the order of the tubes, the judge throws a die two times, resulting in a two-digit number. This number is then looked for in a sorting diagram (see Figure 6.12), and then the tubes are placed on each board in the order given by that number. The top line of the diagram represents the first board and the one under it is the order for the second board.

Before each sorting test, the handler gives the scent of the control person to the dog. After the dog has correctly found and retrieved the control person's tube at each of the two sorting banks, the handler gets the jar with the suspect's tube and then gives that

11 AXBECFD CDXFABE	21 EDBXCAF DCAFBEX	31 BADXCFE DEBFCXA
12 DEXABFC BAFDCEX	22 BCXDAFE EBCDFAX	32 CEBXAFD CABEXDF
13 EBXCFAD CEBAFDX	23 EBCFXAD ABFCXDE	33 EDCFXAB FBAXEDC
14 EXABFCD BEAFXCD	24 BCXAFED AEBCXFD	34 XABFCDE FCDEAXB
15 FEDBCXA BCAEXFD	25 DFABEXC XDFCEBA	35 BXADCEF AXFEDCB
16 XCBAFDE ADXFCEB	26 FBCXEAD BFEDCXA	36 DCFBEXA ADFXBCE
41 CFXEBAD AXBCFED	51 XFDCBEA CAXFDBE	61 FACXBDE XABFDEC
42 DEBFACX XABCFDE	52 XABCEFD FEAXBDC	62 BXFCEDA EFBACDX
43 FEDABCX BEXDCAF	53 CBADXFE XFECADB	63 ACBFXDE DXEBCFA
44 DXBFACE BCDAEXF	54 ABCDEFX DCXBAFE	64 ADFEBXC XBCAEFD
45 XEFBACD BADXFEC	55 EACBDFX DEFXBAC	65 CEADXBF EXBCDAF
46 FEXABCD CDEFABX	56 CDEXFBA ECFADXB	66 ACEBDXF DXBFECA

Figure 6.12 A sorting diagram like this one ensures the placement of the suspect scent is always random.

scent to the dog. The dog must then again investigate the first board for that scent, retrieve it, and then receive the scent again so she can find the match at the second board.

Way of sorting out: 4 × 15 points = 60 points

Way of retrieving: 4 × 5 points = 20 points

General obedience: 10 points

Presentation: 10 points

Maximum score: 100 points

The dog must score at least 80 points to get the Scent Discrimination B Certificate, and to receive a certificate *met lof* (with honors), the dog must receive at least 90 points in total.[13]

RUBBLE SEARCH A

For this certificate, the dog must search for two hidden people in a rubble-covered area that is about 1000 square meters (3281 ft^2). She has 15 minutes to complete the search all by herself and obviously alert (e.g., by barking, scratching, or trying to penetrate the debris). To succeed, she must find and alert for both hidden people.

Dog handler's behavior: 10 points
Way of searching: 30 points
Way of alerting for two people: 2 × 30 points = 60 points
General obedience: 10 points
Presentation: 10 points
Maximum score: 120 points

The dog must score at least 96 points to get the Rubble Search A Certificate, and to receive a certificate *met lof* (with honors), she must score a total of at least 108 points.

RUBBLE SEARCH B

To gain this certification, the dog has 30 minutes to search a rubble-covered area spanning approximately 3000 square meters (9842.5 ft^2) for three hidden people. Again, the dog must search all by herself and observably alert (e.g., bark, scratch, and/or try to penetrate the debris). The search is carried out over the course of two laps with a minimum 30-minute pause, and with at least one of the hidden people being moved from the original hiding place. Distraction is provided by means of a smoldering fire, engine noise, hammer hits, drum sounds, and so on, alongside the rubble-covered area. To succeed, the dog must find and alert for all three hidden people.

Dog handler's behavior: 10 points
Way of searching: 30 points
Way of alerting for three people: 3 × 30 points = 90 points
Total first lap: 130 points

Figure 6.13 To gain her Rubble Search A Certificate, the dog must search for two hidden people in a rubble-covered area that is about 1000 square meters (3281 ft^2). She has 15 minutes to complete the search. For Rubble Search B, the dog must search for three hidden people in a rubble-covered area that is about 3000 square meters (9842.5 ft^2) and locate those people within 30 minutes. Here, one of the authors, Dr. Resi Gerritsen, begins a rubble search with her young Malinois Halusetha's All Power.

Total second lap: 130 points

General obedience: 10 points

Presentation: 10 points

Maximum score: 280 points

The dog must score at least 224 points to get the Rubble Search B Certificate, and to receive a certificate *met lof* (with honors), the dog must score a total of at least 252 points.

AREA SEARCH A

For this certificate, the dog must search for two hidden people in a partially covered and partially open area of 10,000–15,000 square meters (32,808.4–49212.6 ft^2). She has 20 minutes to independently find and alert for the people, using barking, bringsel, or recall. The handler may only walk forward from the starting point, keeping to an imaginary line. During the exam, a person with his leashed dog walks at one of the sides of the area, and at about the same position as the handler. To succeed, the dog must find and alert for both hidden people.

The dog handler's behavior: 10 points
Way of searching: 30 points
Way of alerting for two people: 2 × 30 points = 60 points
General obedience: 10 points
Presentation: 10 points
Maximum score: 120 points

The dog must score at least 96 points to get the Area Search A Certificate, and to receive a certificate *met lof* (with honors), the dog must receive at least a total of 108 points.

THE DIFFERENT ALERTS

1. Barking

    While barking, the dog clearly homes in on the victim or the location of the person's scent. The dog barks continuously in the direction of the found scent until her handler appears and the alert is over. The dog must not touch the found person. When hiding places are enclosed but accessible to the dog, she should indicate the precise location of the scent source by pointing or another direction-giving behavior.

2. Bringsel

    The bringsel is a leather or plastic retrieving tube, approximately as thick as a thumb and, depending on the size of the dog, between 8 and 15 centimeters (3 and 6 in) long. A dog trained to alert with a bringsel wears a collar on which a bringsel is fixed. When she finds a hidden person, the dog grasps the bringsel in her mouth and retrieves it to her handler. There is no need for the dog to sit during the handover of the bringsel. Once the bringsel has been removed—or, in the case of a so-called, "Norwegian bringsel" both the collar and the bringsel—and at the order of the handler, the dog takes the handler directly and independently to the found person.

3. Recall

    If the dog alerts by using recall, after finding a hidden person, she takes the quickest route back and forth between handler and victim, thereby leading the handler to the victim or the place of alert. In addition, the dog must show the handler the sort of behavior that can clearly be interpreted as alert behavior. The dog handler notifies the judge of this type of behavior before the exercise begins.

AREA SEARCH B

For this certificate, the dog has 30 minutes to search and alert for three hidden people in a partially covered and partially open area of 20,000–30,000 square meters (65,618.8–98,425.2 ft^2). She must do this independently and alert in an observable manner (e.g., by barking, bringsel, or recall). The search is carried out in two laps with a minimum 30-minute pause, and all hidden people are moved from their original spots. During the exam, a person with a leashed dog walks along one side of the search area, and in around the same position as the handler. To succeed, the dog must find and alert for all three hidden people.

The dog handler's behavior: 10 points
Way of searching: 30 points
Way of alerting for three people: 3 × 30 points = 90 points
Total first lap: 130 points
Total second lap: 130 points
General obedience: 10 points
Presentation: 10 points
Maximum score: 280 points

Figure 6.14 This picture shows the authors' dog Google. Her harness identifies her as a mission-ready area search dog for the Austrian Red Cross.

The dog must score at least 224 points to get the Area Search B Certificate, and to receive a certificate *met lof* (with honors), she must receive at least a total of 252 points.[14]

Cadaver Search Dogs

Cadaver search dogs have been widely used around the world for many years. In cases where a dead body will be the likely outcome of a search action, cadaver search dogs, rather than SAR dogs, are used to search for human remains. This is because a SAR dog is trained to find living humans. Cadaver search dogs are trained to locate and follow the scent of decomposing human bodies and are the ideal tools to assist law enforcement officers in the gruesome

Figure 6.15 In cases where a dead body will be the likely outcome of a search action, cadaver search dogs are used to find human remains. Cadaver search dogs, here a Dutch Police dog, are trained to locate and follow the scent of decomposing human remains, even if the remains have been buried for years and are deep underground or have been lying at the bottom of a lake (or another body of water) for some time. (*Onze Hond*/KLPD)

and arduous task of searching for human remains. The cadaver search dog's job is not only vital to the justice system that often needs a body to prove a crime, but also to the families of the victims, who seek closure.

These dogs are trained to smell decomposition, which means they can locate body parts, tissue, blood, and bone. They can also detect residue scents, so they can tell if a body has been somewhere, even if it's not there anymore. This is not rocket science for dogs, who all know where they last buried a bone because of such residues. They are trained to detect the scent of human decomposition that rises from the soil and can work on and off leash.

In our training, we always use human remains, available to professionals in the Netherlands. There are some substitute, commercially available odors (the most common is Sigma Pseudo Corpse Scent, which comes in three varieties: recently dead, decomposed, and drowned), but deceased humans produce unique volatile organic compounds, and dogs have a keenly attuned sense

Figure 6.16 Cadaver search dogs are specially trained to find the scent of human decomposition in the air. Such search dogs, like this one that works for the Belgian Federal Police, also detect residue scents: they can tell if a body has been in a place, even if it's not there anymore. (Belgian Federal Police, www.polfed-fedpol.be)

of smell, so you should practice only with the real thing. Always keep in mind that until proved otherwise, every area is a crime scene. Train your dog to sit or lie down when she locates a scent's source. Digging, peeing, and excited behavior can destroy important evidence.

Cadaver search dogs can be used to detect buried human remains that result from a crime or natural disaster, as well as human remains concealed in bodies of water, both on the surface and submerged. Water search dogs or submerged-body detection dogs search large areas of water, both lakes and rivers, and can perform searches of these environments in approximately 10 percent of the time taken by dogs using other recognized search techniques.

Ore Deposit Dogs

Ore deposit dogs are trained to find mineral deposits because many mineral ores—especially sulfide ores such as zinc, copper, or nickel—emit a specific aroma that a dog can be trained to detect. In the spring of 1962, Finnish professors A. Kahma and T. Mustonen wondered if dogs could smell a rock containing sulfide ore. As most geologists worldwide had noticed, sulfides emit an odor, especially when broken. They contacted late Mr. Pentti Mattsson, a well know Finnish dog trainer, and asked if it would be possible to train a dog to smell ore. Mattsson started training his dog Lari with pyrite boulders and soon Kahma and Mustonen organized some experiments, with which the dog coped very well. Even in the winter, while braving freezing weather and deep snow, the dog found chalcopyrite boulders under the snow. The scientists' belief in the dog's skills strengthened. The Geological Survey of Finland used 16 prospecting dogs between 1964 and 1994 to detect sulfide-containing boulders. By the mid-1980s, eight dogs were being used to detect ore deposits in Finland.

The training methods for prospecting dogs are based on Pentti Mattsson's results, obtained through experiments. In one test conducted in Virtasalmi in 1965, in an area covering over 9 square kilometers (5.6 mi^2), Mattsson's dog found 1330 boulders containing sulfide, whereas the boulder prospector managed to find only 270 boulders, even though he knew he was competing against the dog. The ore detection dogs were most effective at finding sulfide-bearing rocks, including chalcopyrite, galena, molybdenum, pyrite, and pyrrhotite. Based on Mattsson's example and training methods, the training of the world's first drug detection dogs began in the United Kingdom.

The Finnish dogs' effective working time was about six years and the fieldwork period was about six months per year. The costs incurred by a prospecting dog consist mainly of the dog trainer's salary and maintenance costs. The dogs proved most valuable after a boulder discovery when they could quickly find more boulders to trace the source. Dogs played a role locating several large ore and mineral deposits. In 1994, even though the overall results had been quite good, use of dogs was considered too expensive and discontinued.

In 2012, Swedish geologist Peter Bergman started the Swedish company OreDog to help find mine locations with ore dogs. Bergman stated his dog could sense 20 to 30 different types of ore and as deep as 12 meters (30 ft) underground.

Drug Detection Dogs

A drug detection dog is trained to use her senses, mainly smell, to detect a variety of drug substances (e.g., cocaine, heroin, LSD, marijuana, methamphetamines, MDMA, PCP, and others). She is trained to locate and pinpoint drug odor sources of varying sizes, from residual amounts to large trafficking quantities. Drug detection dogs can be trained to an active (e.g., scratching, barking) or passive (e.g., sitting, lying down) alert. Many law enforcement agencies, as well as commercial detection businesses, prefer the passive alert to avoid damage to vehicles and other property.

Detector dogs, including drug detector dogs, have no interest in the item they are searching for—what they're searching for is their favorite toy. Their training has led them to associate that toy with the smell of drugs (or ore, or whatever it is they've been trained to find). Detector dogs all use their hunting instinct to search for what they've been trained to find. They know that once they've found and alerted for the substance their handlers are looking for, they will be rewarded with their toy.

Drug detection dogs work wherever people, goods, and mail enter or leave a country, including harbors and international airports. Besides border security work, they also work in mail centers, and they regularly search ships, small craft, and cargo. The drug detection dog is the most cost effective, least invasive, and most visible line of defense in the battle to keep drugs out of workplaces, music festivals, and other big events.[15]

Figure 6.17 Drug detection dogs work wherever people, goods, and mail enter or leave a country, including harbors and international airports. Besides border security work, they also work in mail centers, and they regularly search ships, small craft, and cargo. This dog belonging to the Dutch Royal Marechaussee works at Schiphol Amsterdam Airport. (*Onze Hond* Archive)

DRUG SUSPICION CONFIRMED

The key turns in the lock, and the dog handler pushes the door open. We are in the hallway of a dilapidated building that will soon be torn down. The interiors are surprisingly clean. Until recently this place was still inhabited, and the electricity works. The handler wonders if his Malinois, Ann, will find any narcotics when she searches the building. He can hear her barking impatiently as she waits in the car. But before he goes to get Ann, he first goes through all the rooms in the house to get an overview.

We go up the creaky wooden stairs. It smells a little stale. All the floors are made of smooth wood or stone. While touring the building, the handler tells us Ann is trained to recognize all commercially popular drugs. "On the street, however, almost every week, new combinations of speed, ecstasy, and crack come out. These drugs are synthetic and absolutely odorless for humans, but Ann can smell them."

The tour complete, the handler lets Ann out of the car. She cannot wait to get started. With a deep nose she examines the wall along every nook and cranny. She's quick, and she nervously moves her tail. When we get to the kitchen, Ann searches both the ground and above. Her search is systematic, and nothing escapes her attention. She puts her front paws up on the refrigerator to smell at the lamp on the ceiling, goes back and sniffs the doorknob, and then sniffs the table and shelves. Two or three times she turns, always coming back to the stove. Suddenly, she begins scraping vigorously at the stove door. Excited, she barks. A clear, reliable indication.

The handler cautiously opens the door, simultaneously dropping Ann's favorite toy. Proudly, Ann retrieves her toy and trots a lap of honor around the kitchen. Ann's suspicion has been confirmed.

In the stove, among ashes, we see empty packages of narcotics that are only slightly singed, as well as partially fused plastic bags. Many empty drug packages. Suspicion of a large drug-trafficking activity against the two accused is likely to be confirmed. For safety's sake, Ann conducts one last search of the house before we start the next search: a suspect's farm.

Explosive and Mine Detection Dogs

For many years, dogs have saved human lives by warning their handlers of explosive devices. They work with the police and military to locate dangerous materials and are trained to detect at least 12 basic odors, which allows them to sense improvised explosive devices (IEDs) and other types and compositions of explosives. The dogs may be trained to recognize chemicals, such as ammonium nitrate, potassium chlorate, potassium and sodium nitrate; high explosives, such as TNT, PETN-based explosives, RDX-based explosives, and dynamite; and low explosives, such as black powder, smokeless powder, and other pyrotechnic compositions.

The dogs go through an intense training regime to learn how to locate and identify a wide variety of explosives and how to alert their handlers of their presence. Training also includes search patterns for buildings outside and inside, vehicles, parcels, luggage, open areas, and airplanes. Explosive detection dogs are

Figure 6.18 Explosive detection dogs go through an intense training course to learn how to locate and identify a wide variety of explosives and to alert their handlers to their presence. Training also includes search patterns for buildings, parcels, luggage, open areas, airplanes, and vehicles. This dog works for the Belgian Federal Police. (Belgian Federal Police, www.polfed-fedpol.be)

used for cargo inspections and other preventive searches (also called bomb checks); searches in response to bomb threats; and specific searches for fireworks, firearms, and/or ammunition. Dogs can also be trained to detect bombs, especially for roadside bomb-detection work.[16]

EXPLOSIVES BETWEEN TIN AND PEPPER

While the Rotterdam police trained their dogs, we were able to train our explosive detector dogs in the century-old warehouses in that city's port. Since the 17th century, tin and pepper have been stored in these warehouses with beautiful names like Celebes, Borneo, Java, and Sumatra. One training night, the instructor hid different types of explosives and weapons between the massive tin rods and giant bales of pepper. Ruud and his Malinois Eva and the young dog Speedy, as well as Ruud's colleagues and their dogs, searched the warehouses for the contraband. The overwhelming scent of pepper and tin proved to be no problem for the dogs, who detected the hidden weaponry and explosives within a relatively short time of beginning the search. When Ruud came home that evening and the dogs enthusiastically greeted Resi, she immediately began to sneeze and cried out in astonishment, "Oh, you all stink of pepper!" It was indeed surprising that despite the pepper's masking scent, the dogs did their jobs so well.

Accelerant Detection Dogs

Every year, money, property, and lives are lost due to arson. An accelerant detection dog, also called an arson dog, is trained to search quickly and accurately for minute traces of accelerants that may have been used to start fires, even tiny amounts of anything from lamp oil to lighter fluid in a scene flooded with several inches of water or covered in snow, ice, mud, or thick layers of debris. These dogs go through extensive training before becoming certified accelerant detection dogs, and their handlers are law enforcement officers trained to investigate fire scenes.

Arson dogs can detect substances such as acetone, brake fluid, charcoal starter fluid, Coleman fuel, diesel, gasoline, lighter fluid, naphtha, thinner, turpentine, and other fuel sources that can be used to start fires.

Figure 6.19 Accelerant detection dogs, also called arson dogs, can survey a variety of terrain in a fire scene in an incredibly short time. In doing so, they dramatically increase the handler's ability to get an accurate sense of the flammable products present in a fire scene and increase the chances of collecting a positive sample of an accelerant. (Belgian Federal Police, www.polfed-fedpol.be)

Arson dogs survey a variety of terrains in a fire scene in an incredibly short time, dramatically increasing their handlers' ability to get an accurate picture of the flammable products present and increase the chances of collecting a positive sample.

Mold Detection Dogs

Mold detection dogs, sometimes called rothounds, search inside buildings for fungi that cause decay and deterioration of timber. One of these fungi is *Serpula lacrymans*, also called dry rot, which flourishes where there is moisture. It is related to mushroom and toadstool fungi, and has a distinctly mushroomy odor. By the time people detect this smell, it is already producing masses of mycelium and fungal fruiting bodies. When fungi have reached this stage, they are likely to have caused considerable damage to affected timbers. Mold detection dogs, which can detect the odor of the fungi before people can, should be brought in early if dry rot is suspected. Mold detection dogs can also be trained to search for other fungi, and they may have to work in areas of buildings that are many hundreds of years old. The dogs must not only be able to detect the fungus but also how far it has spread. They locate its source so that treatment can begin in the correct location. Dogs can also access places that are difficult for humans to reach and can cover a large surface area to find concealed mold.

Mold detection dogs are first trained to hunt for toys, and then scent is added to the toy. The toy is then taken away, so the dog is only working with the scent of the mold in an affected area. Detecting the smell of mold is part of a game for these dogs, and they always receive a reward once they have detected the scent. In real search actions, mold detection dogs point to the infected area, and then humans inspect the area, taking samples and then drawing up remediation plans for the building.

Figure 6.20 Mold detection dogs, sometimes called rothounds, search buildings for fungi that cause decay and deterioration of timber. The dogs sometimes work in areas of buildings that are many hundreds of years old, and their skills are not only used to detect fungi but also how far it has spread. (*Onze Hond* Archive)

Bed Bug–Detector Dogs

Bed bugs (*Cimex lectularius*) can become a major problem for businesses, hotels, and homeowners, so a new employee has entered the workforce to stop them: who else but the dog, with her excellent nose? The brown-colored bed bugs can be hard to find and identify because of their small size and habit of staying hidden. Exterminators and business owners enlist the dog's incredible abilities to find where bed bugs are hiding. Dogs are also vital for follow-up, to determine if an extermination method has worked. Today, professional groups have established standards in bed bug–detector dog training, testing, and certification.

Currency Detection Dogs

Currency detection dogs are trained to detect large amounts of concealed money, mostly dollars and euro notes. The dogs are trained to give either a passive or active alert. If one of these dogs detects concealed currency on a person, she will follow and block the suspect. These dogs are also trained to search airplanes and airports, agricultural areas and open yards, buildings, lockers, luggage, packages, open areas, ships and harbors, and vehicles.

Figure 6.21 Since 2010, European customs agencies have used dogs to detect large amounts of cash. The dogs are usually trained to detect packages of 100 or more banknotes. (*Onze Hond* Archive)

MONEY DOESN'T SMELL, OR DOES IT?

Tail wagging, panting, and continuously looking back to her handler, the Malinois Aska walks through the crowd. Fast and targeted, her nose scans pants, suitcases, and backpacks. Sometimes she quickly rises on her hind legs to smell a shirt—paying close attention to a breast pocket or inner pocket—without touching the person wearing it. With a calm hand gesture, Aska's handler guides her. Some passengers look afraid and some are afraid and hold their hands high. When she reaches a large man carrying a suitcase and briefcase, Aska pushes forward enthusiastically, tail wagging, her nose resolutely at work. With continuous glances up at her handler, Aska sits down at the man's feet. The handler quickly gives her a reward, and when he appeals to the man, the man nods and confesses that he has a lot of money with him.

Four-year-old Aska is trained to recognize the smell of money, a unique combination of special paper and banknote ink, and works especially on flights that are analyzed by customs as "risk flights," those with the greatest chance of carrying suspect money.

Oil and Gas Detection Dogs

The main reasons for incidents and disruption on pipelines are excavation damage to the pipeline, illegal pipeline tapping, or corrosion of steel pipes. Almost all pipelines under or above Earth's

Figure 6.22 Some detector dogs are trained to find power failures in underground cables and pipes. The dogs smell the combustion gases that result in cables if there is a malfunction. Even up to three days after a problem, a trained dog can indicate the spot underground where the malfunction occurred. (*Onze Hond* Archive)

surface, long and short, remote or near human settlements, are accessible to detecting dogs; dogs can easily investigate forests, mountains, and rural areas or fields with dense vegetation, where many measuring instruments cannot be used. In the dog, oil and gas industry companies have an effective, efficient, and safe detecting tool that works with speed and accuracy.

Gas detection dogs search for gas leaks in pipelines and valves located above or below Earth's surface and can identify the location of gas leaks in environments contaminated by gas. These dogs are trained to detect gases that do not occur freely in nature or in human communities. Natural gas detection dogs, therefore, are not trained to detect methane, as methane is a freely occurring substance. It's important for these dogs to be sensitive only to substances exclusive to pipelines; the customer does not want to pay for unnecessary excavation work.

Figure 6.23 Illegal cell phones in the possession of prison inmates pose a security threat, and they are among the biggest problems prison officials face. Psychologist Stanley Coren wrote that he left a collection of cell-phone parts in airtight glass boxes for 10 days. When he opened them, even his human nose could detect a "sweet metallic smell." If we can detect them, dogs certainly can! Here, Kyra of the Dutch Dog Training Center, Oosterhout, shows what she has found during a short search period. (Dog Training Center, Oosterhout)

Detecting leaks in gas and oil pipelines in early stages is crucial to guarantee both quality and continuity of pipeline infrastructure. Oil detection dogs are powerful helpers in locating leaks on active oil lines before the oil contaminates waterways or farmers' fields and groundwater. One of the advantages of using detection dogs for oil and gas leaks is their ability to quickly detect tiny amounts of the substances they are trained to recognize, even parts per billion, which helps pipeline operators prevent potential hazardous-substance accidents.

New Detecting Dog Tasks

It is impossible for us to include all the tasks in which the modern Malinois plays an important role. In addition to the jobs noted above, Malinois are also employed in tobacco detection, searching for illegal tobacco; medical detection, searching for illnesses such as cancer in humans; biosecurity detection, helping to protect countries from exotic pests and diseases from agricultural sources; cell phone detection, searching for the hottest contraband for prison inmates (both the phones themselves and items concealed in the phones), which are difficult to detect because of their size.

Conclusion

A Lack of Character

First-time dog owners often have few demands of their dogs: their pets must be "very lovable" and, of course, "obedient." They must also be "alert." Furthermore, these pet owners absolutely do not want "character" dogs (by which they mean stubborn, dominant, or overactive dogs) because they are so difficult to educate.

Unfortunately, many of the dog breeds that are popular with the public have up until now been working dogs: sheepdogs, guard dogs, and protection dogs, all of which, historically, have been character dogs that hold their ground in most situations. But the average pet owner wants a lovable, devoted pet—even if he or she has just picked out a Belgian shepherd at a local kennel.

The public will get what they ask for. Over the past 40 years, many breeds that up until recently were dependable working dogs have become, through thoughtless breeding, nervous salon dogs. This fits the demands of the modern pet owner very well, because nervous and frightened dogs firmly press themselves on their owners and are therefore considered "very loving." Due to their excessive submissiveness, they are most of the time slavishly servile to people, and are therefore taken to be "obedient." And because

Figure 7.01 If we want our grandchildren to know working dogs that still have their original character, we need to protect working-dog lines. Here, the authors' grandson Joran with their Malinois Google van het Eldenseveld.

these dogs are afraid of even their own shadows, every sound will make them bark, so the proud owners conclude they are "alert" guard dogs. For sure, they bark and are lovable and obedient. But for completely different reasons than their forebears.

Breed Foundations

Required practical qualities of a dog breed were, and still are, the baseline for many breed standards, and therefore the foundation of most breeds. When we allow ourselves to undermine those foundations, we do so knowing that the sturdy buildings our predecessors constructed will eventually fall. Some might say, "The practical value of my breed doesn't interest me. I have my dog only as a nice pet, and I don't want to train him. Besides, many standards suggest that my dog's breed is an ideal pet." In some ways, this is correct, but the sentiment is wrong. We must watch that we don't throw the baby out with the bathwater.

There are many gun dogs out there that have never seen game or retrieved a bird. By the same token, there are many sheepdogs that stalk sheep instead of tending them, or guard and protection dogs that have not the slightest idea how to defend against an attack. We must not interpret the breed standards too literally. At the same time, we should not disregard the practical value of modern dogs. Indeed, it isn't necessary that every gun dog, shepherd, or guard dog individually performs the work he was originally bred for. On principle, though, it is desirable that the breeding lines stay mentally and physically suitable for their original work, even if some of these dogs will never be working dogs.

Breed Characteristics

Even a dog with a serious fault to his breed standard can be a fine dog and will without any doubt be an unforgettable friend. But the love of our own dogs should not blind us to what the breed must be. All breeds should have their own character, a certain behavior, a certain structure, and characteristics that have a direct connection with the original work our predecessors selected those dogs for, sometimes centuries ago. Those specific qualities demarcate the specific breeds, leave their marks on them, and should be inseparably connected to them. A terrier has a different structure and temperament than a sheepdog because, originally, the two breeds did completely different things. It is crucial that we do not damage that careful selection in the space of a few years.

With the dilution of working qualities, the dog himself, in creature, character, and type, becomes diluted. If people really want to have a "uniform" sort of dog, we had better breed a new "family" dog for them. But such people, and breeders working for those people, should stay away from working dogs. Fortunately, there are still enough people out there who appreciate the working dog, with all his distinctive characteristics.

We have more need for beautiful dogs that have stable characters than beautiful but mentally weak and inferior dogs. We must not turn the whole ship around to custom fit breeds according to the desires of pet buyers. The different dog breeds once demanded certain requirements of character and therefore certain types of owners, not the other way around!

The Malinois

In all the working dog breeds we have known—the giant schnauzer, Doberman, Rottweiler, Bouvier des Flandres, and even the German shepherd—poor breeding with bad combinations, and breeding mainly for beauty, means that today only a few breeds remain as reliable service dogs. Worldwide, the Malinois is now working dog number one. But what if by today's careless breeding in the future we lose the strong Malinois character, and thus an excellent tool in important customs, military, and police duties? Please, let's keep our eyes open, and keep our Malinois dogs' characters intact.

Appendix

KNPV National Champions, 1946–2017

Following is a list of the KNPV National Champions—PH-1, PH-2 (beginning in 1959), and Object Guarding (beginning in 1978)—starting with 2017 and going back to 1946. Remember, dogs may only participate in the annual KNPV PH-1 championship once; after that, they must participate in PH-2.

2017 – PH-1: xMalinois Spike with handler R.J.D. Coolen; PH-2: xDutch shepherd Spike with handler I.P.T. Janssen; Object Guarding: Malinois Darco with handler E. van Rey

2016 – PH-1: German shepherd dog Enzo van de Wiersdijk with handler R.A.J.G. Verbruggen; PH-2: xDutch shepherd dog Spike with handler I.P.T. Janssen; Object Guarding: xMalinois dog Pepper with handler J. Broekhuizen

2015 – PH-1: xMalinois dog Mack with handler W. Pisters; PH-2: xMalinois dog Jagger with handler J. Delissen; Object Guarding: xMalinois dog Directeur with handler A. Kleine Schaars

2014 – PH-1: xMalinois bitch Annie with handler H.R. Iedema; PH-2: xMalinois dog Senna with handler A.C. Gravemaker;

Object Guarding: xMalinois dog Glenn with handler M.J. van Ginkel

2013 – PH-1: xMalinois dog Roy with handler H. Pegge; PH-2: xMalinois dog Rudy Jr. with handler J. Seegers; Object Guarding: xMalinois dog Ferdi with handler S. van Zuijlekom

2012 – PH-1: German shepherd dog Arras with handler R. Cordong; PH-2: xDutch shepherd dog Greagus with handler D. van den Brink; Object Guarding: xMalinois dog Lucas with handler B. Donker

2011 – PH-1: xDutch shepherd dog Nero with handler C.M.J. Barents; PH-2: xMalinois dog Django with handler J.J. van Oetelaar; Object Guarding: xMalinois dog Sheriff with handler K.J. Sterk

2010 – PH-1: xDutch shepherd dog Boy with handler L. Hawinkels; PH-2: xDutch shepherd dog Rex with handler R. Cordong; Object Guarding: xMalinois dog Dorus with handler A. Kleine Schaars

2009 – PH-1: xMalinois dog Django with handler J.J. van den Oetelaar; PH-2: xMalinois dog Mike with handler W.H.M. Kranen; Object Guarding: xMalinois dog Vico with handler A.A.C. van de Moosdijk

2008 – PH-1: xMalinois dog Baron with handler H.A.G. Bolster; PH-2: xMalinois dog Rudy with handler M.H.E. Janssen; Object Guarding: xMalinois dog Chico with handler J.T.H.M Willems

2007 – PH-1: xMalinois dog Rex with handler P. Kepers; PH-2: tied, xMalinois dog Rudy with handler M.H.E. Janssen and xMalinois dog Bowy with handler J. Tuin; Object Guarding: German shepherd xMalinois dog Arras with handler E. Walda

2006 – PH-1: tied, xDutch shepherd dog Tim with handler A.H.M. Groothuys and xMalinois dog Alex with handler C.J.G. van

Nistelrooy; PH-2: xMalinois dog Beau with handler H.A.G. Bolster; Object Guarding: xMalinois dog Jary with handler M.M. Endevoets

2005 – PH-1: Malinois dog Roy with handler L. Beck; PH-2 and Object Guarding: xMalinois dog Beau with handler H.A.G. Bolster

2004 – PH-1: Malinois dog Rudie with handler N.P.C. Seegers; PH-2: Malinois bitch Cobra with handler L.J. Beck-Schipper; Object Guarding: Malinois dog Rocco with handler A. Kamps

2003 – PH-1: Malinois dog Eddy with handler A.H.M. Groothuys; PH-2: Dutch shepherd dog Kazan with handler L. Beck; Object Guarding: tied, Malinois bitch Cobra with handler L.J. Beck-Schipper and Malinois dog Xanti with handler W.H.M. Walda-van Stiphout

2002 – PH-1: Malinois dog Chris with handler J. Janssen; PH-2: Dutch shepherd dog Nico van Neerland with handler J. Huiting; Object Guarding: Malinois bitch Jessie with handler P. te Pas

2001 – PH-1: Malinois dog Kazan with handler L. Beck; PH-2: Malinois bitch Kelly with handler G.A.J. van Hagen; Object Guarding: Malinois dog Quatro with handler M.G.H. Peeters

2000 – PH-1: Malinois bitch Linsy with handler A.H.M. Groothuis; PH-2: Malinois dog Laron with handler H.C. Roelofs; Object Guarding: Malinois dog Danny with handler F.H. Wirsching

1999 – PH-1: Malinois dog Marco with handler G. van Vemde; PH-2: Malinois dog Huub with handler A.L. Kok; Object Guarding: Malinois dog Rocky with handler R. Schotkamp

1998 – PH-1: Malinois dog Tjek with handler N. Poen; PH-2: Malinois dog Laron with handler H.C. Roelofs; Object

Guarding: Malinois dog Bico with handler H.C.M. Timmermans

1997 – PH-1: Malinois dog Roy with handler J. van Beek; PH-2: Malinois dog Laron with handler H.C. Roelofs; Object Guarding: Groenendael dog Eros with handler J.L. van Dijk

1996 – PH-1: Malinois dog Rocky with handler H.G. Pegge; PH-2: Malinois dog Laron with handler H.C. Roelofs; Object Guarding: Malinois dog Buck with handler P. Mandemaker

1995 – PH-1: Malinois dog Bruno with handler C.B. van der Steen; PH-2: Malinois dog Zacko with handler R.W. Stuurman; Object Guarding: Malinois dog Laron with handler H.C. Roelofs

1994 – PH-1: Malinois dog Faston with handler J.M. Lourensen; PH-2: Malinois dog Zacko with handler R.W. Stuurman; Object Guarding: Malinois dog Ducky with handler C.H.M. Beysterveldt

1993 – PH-1: Malinois dog Rudo with handler J.R. van Vulpen; PH-2: Malinois bitch Donna with handler K. Terpstra; Object Guarding: German shepherd dog Tarzan with handler T.J.G. Peters

1992 – PH-1: Malinois dog Rico with handler H.R. Iedema; PH-2: Malinois bitch Donna with handler K. Terpstra; Object Guarding: Malinois dog Iron with handler H. C. Roelofs

1991 – PH-1: Malinois dog Berry with handler E. Geytebeek; PH-2: Malinois bitch Donna with handler K. Terpstra; Object Guarding: Malinois dog Benji with handler J.H. Thijsen

1990 – PH-1: Malinois dog Basco with handler J. van den Oetelaar; PH-2 and Object Guarding: Malinois dog Rambo with handler J.H. van Rossum

1989 – PH-1: Malinois bitch Laika with handler N. van Oosterhout; PH-2: Malinois dog Madjoe with handler R. van der Velde;

Object Guarding: Malinois dog Berry with handler J.A. Hogeling

1988 – PH-1: Malinois dog Rudy with handler P. Sommers; PH-2: Malinois dog Madjoe with handler R. van der Velde; Object Guarding: Malinois dog Speedy with handler J.L.H. Tinnemans

1987 – PH-1: Malinois dog Roy with handler R. Epping; PH-2: Malinois dog Victor with handler H. Smits; Object Guarding: Dutch shepherd dog Robbie with handler J.H. van Rossum

1986 – PH-1: Malinois bitch Sascha with handler A. Jansen; PH-2 and Object Guarding: Malinois dog Nero with handler L.G.M. Jansen

1985 – PH-1: Malinois dog Berry with handler J.A. Hogeling; PH-2: Malinois dog Kwint with handler G.J. Duinkerk; Object Guarding: Malinois dog Marco with handler T. Kleine Schaars

1984 – PH-1: Malinois dog Tim with handler A.H.M. Groothuis; PH-2: Malinois dog Voltan with handler H.J. Vossen; Object Guarding: Malinois dog Marco with handler J.B.N.M. Colaris

1983 – PH-1: Groenendael dog Nero with handler Th. Berkers; PH-2: Malinois dog Rudy with handler W.H. Rijvers; Object Guarding: Malinois dog Benno with handler L.J.J. Habraken

1982 – PH-1: Malinois dog Tarzan with handler J. Boele; PH-2: Malinois dog Marco with handler J.H. Kok; Object Guarding: Malinois dog Boy with handler J.H. Verrips

1981 – PH-1: Malinois dog Karlos with handler M. Styvers; PH-2: Malinois dog Marco with handler H. Bongaerts; Object Guarding: Malinois dog Duco with handler W. de Ruiter

1980 – PH-1: Malinois bitch Tanja with handler P. Klotz; PH-2: Groenendael dog Andor van de Ijsselvloed with handler Th. Berkers; Object Guarding: Malinois dog Leon with handler P.M.A. van der Berg

1979 – PH-1: Malinois dog Ronnie with handler A.R.L. Massop; PH-2: Groenendael dog Andor van de Ijsselvloed with handler Th. Berkers; Object Guarding: Malinois dog Prins with handler R. Koster

1978 – PH-1: Malinois dog Carlo with handler A.A. Lamers; PH-2: Malinois dog Nero with handler A. Kamps; the first National Championship in Object Guarding: Bouvier des Flandres bitch Stella with handler Th. G. Janssen

1977 – PH-1: Malinois Nero with handler A. Kamps; PH-2: Groenendael Andor van de Ijsselvloed with handler Th. Berkers

1976 – PH-1: Malinois Robbie with handler H.J. Lennertz; PH-2: Malinois Nero with handler P.V.M. Klotz

1975 – PH-1: Malinois Leon with handler J.H. Thijssen; PH-2: Malinois Robbie with handler A.C.T. Hoogenboom

1974 – PH-1: Dutch shepherd Tarzan with handler M.H. Linkens; PH-2: Malinois Roland with handler A. Bijl

1973 – PH-1: Malinois Wilson with handler A.J. Verhagen; PH-2: Malinois Linda with handler H. van Es

1972 – PH-1: Malinois Roland with handler G.L.J. Berkelaar; PH-2: Malinois Cabil with handler H.J. Lennertz

1971 – PH-1: Malinois Marco with handler P. van Oosterhout; PH-2: Bouvier des Flandres Lex with handler A.B. Verheijen

1970 – PH-1: Malinois Robbie with handler M.M. Linkens; PH-2: Malinois Nero with handler L. Jansen

1969 – PH-1: Malinois Marco with handler J.H. Wekers; PH-2: Malinois Nero with handler L. Jansen

1968 – PH-1: Malinois Arno with handler L. Jansen; PH-2: Malinois Nero with handler L. Jansen

1967 – PH-1: German shepherd dog Castor with handler W. Geisberts; PH-2: Malinois Nero with handler L. Jansen

1966 – PH-1: German shepherd dog Arno with handler F. Slaats; PH-2: Belgian shepherd Astor with handler T. Prins

1965 – PH-1: Dutch shepherd Leo with handler S. van Houwelingen; PH-2: Malinois Blitz with handler N. Sweres

1964 – PH-1: Bouvier des Flandres Robbie with handler H.J.Wijnen; PH-2: Bouvier des Flandres Donar with handler P. van Oosterhout

1963 – PH-1: German shepherd dog Kazan with handler A.M. van den Bosch; PH-2: Malinois Blitz with handler N. Sweres

1962 – PH-1: Malinois Blitz with handler N. Sweres; PH-2: German shepherd dog Huub with handler A.D. van Lamoen

1961 – PH-1: Malinois Jonny with handler F. Backe; PH-2: Bouvier des Flandres Wibo with handler J. Stroo

1960 – PH-1: Bouvier des Flandres Dona with handler P. van Oosterhout; PH-2: Bouvier des Flandres Hero with handler H. van den Brink

1959 – PH-1: Malinois Arno with handler H.P.H. de Vocht; the first National Championship in PH-2: Bouvier des Flandres Leo with handler G. Otten

1958 – PH-1: Malinois Walter with handler M. Kroot

1957 – PH-1: Bouvier des Flandres Bart with handler M.J. Wouters

1956 – PH-1: Bouvier des Flandres Boy with handler C. Jordaans

1955 – PH-1: Bouvier des Flandres Leo with handler J. Rooyakkers

1954 – PH-1: Bouvier des Flandres Breston with handler W. Veenendaal

1953 – PH-1: Malinois Benno with handler W.G. van Lieshout

1952 – PH-1: Malinois Nero with handler H. Schoenmakers

1951 – PH-1: Dutch shepherd Yorka with handler A. Bakker
1950 – PH-1: Dutch shepherd Nero with handler J. van der Kaa
1949 – PH-1: Dutch shepherd Nero with handler J. van der Kaa
1948 – PH-1: Bouvier des Flandres Benno with handler A.M. van Aggel
1947 – PH-1: Breston with handler H.J. Kranenburg
1946 – PH-1: Bouvier des Flandres Kastor with handler C. Smets

Notes

1 C. Vilà, P. Savolainen, J.E. Maldonado, et al., "Multiple and Ancient Origins of the Domestic Dog," *Science* 276 (1997): 1687–1689, DOI: 10.1126/science.276.5319.1687; C. Vilà, I.R. Amorim, J.A. Leonard, et al., "Mitochondrial DNA Phylogeography and Population History of the Grey Wolf *Canis lupus*," *Molecular Ecology* 8 (1999): 2089–2103. See also: M. Balter, "Burying Man's Best Friend, With Honor," *Science* 329, no. 5998 (1999): 1464–1465, DOI: 10.1126/science.329.5998.1464-b; Adam H. Freedman, et al., "Genome Sequencing Highlights Genes Under Selection and the Dynamic Early History of Dogs," *PLOS Genetics*. PLOS Org. 10, no. 1 (January 16, 2014): DOI: 10.1371/journal.pgen.1004016; G. Larson, D.G. Bradley, "How Much Is That in Dog Years? The Advent of Canine Population Genomics," *PLOS Genetics*. 10, no. 1 (2014): DOI: 10.1371/journal.pgen.1004093.

2 M. Germonpré et al. "Fossil Dogs and Wolves from Palaeolithic Sites in Belgium, the Ukraine and Russia: Osteometry, Ancient DNA and Stable Isotopes." *Journal of Archaeological Science* 36, no. 2 (February 2009): 473–490. See also O. Thalmann et al. "Complete Mitochondrial Genomes of Ancient Canids Suggest a European Origin of Domestic Dogs." *Science* 342, no. 6160 (15 November 2013): 871–874.

3 I.H. Pidoplichko. *Upper Palaeolithic Dwellings of Mammoth Bones in the Ukraine: Kiev-Kirillovskii, Gontsy, Dobranichevka, Mezin and Mezhirich.* Kiev, 1969.

4 R.P. Coppinger, and L. Coppinger, *Dogs: A New Understanding of Canine Origin, Behavior and Evolution* (Chicago: University of Chicago Press, 2001); K. Lorenz, *Man Meets Dog* (Boston: Houghton Mifflin, 1954); F.E. Zeuner, *A History of Domesticated Animals* (New York: Harper and Row, 1963).

5 A reaal is a royal coin made of gold, silver, or copper and used in the Netherlands and Flanders from the 16th to 18th centuries. Its value differed over the years. A ceurreaal has a higher value than a reaal.

6 Charles Estienne, *L'agriculture et Maison Rustique* (Antwerp: Christoffel Plantijn, 1566; reprinted in 1640 in Dutch as *De landtwinninghe ende hoeve*).

7 See Cornelia Kraus, Samuel Pavard, and Daniel E. L. Promislow, "The Size–Life Span Trade-Off Decomposed: Why Large Dogs Die Young," *The American Naturalist*, 181, no. 4 (April 2013).
8 In 1911 the Ter Heide kennel, founded in 1894 by Louis Huyghebaert, had been sold with kennel name, dogs, and all, to Ridder Hynderick de Theulegoet.
9 BBC News, Tayside and Central Scotland, December 29, 2014.
10 Ibid.
11 More information about this unique KNPV program and its training can be found in our book *K9 Personal Protection: A Manual for Training Reliable Protection Dogs* (Brush Education).
12 More information about tracking can be found in our book, *K9 Professional Tracking* (Brush Education).
13 More information about scent-discrimination lineups can be found in our books *K9 Investigation Errors* and *K9 Suspect Discrimination* (Brush Education).
14 More information about search and rescue can be found in our book *K9 Search and Rescue* (Brush Education).
15 More information about drug detection dogs can be found in our book *K9 Drug Detection* (Brush Education).
16 More information about explosive detection dogs can be found in our book *K9 Explosive and Mine Detection* (Brush Education).

Bibliography

Aubry, Jacqueline. *Le Berger Belge*. Volumes 1 & 2. Paris: Editions Crepin-Leblond, 1977 and 1994.

Balter, Michael. "Burying Man's Best Friend, With Honor." *Science* 329, no. 5998 (2010): 1464–5. https://doi.org/10.1126/science.329.5998.1464-b.

Ceulebroeck, Georges V. *L'Histoire du Berger Belge*. Charleroi: self-publication, 1983.

Chasse et Pêche. Belgian cynologique magazine. Editions as noted in text.

Coppinger, Raymond P., and Lorna Coppinger. *Dogs: A New Understanding of Canine Origin, Behavior and Evolution*. Chicago: University of Chicago Press, 2001.

Coren, Stanley. *Phone Sniffing Dogs: A New Weapon Against High Tech Crime*. Psychologytoday.com. December 18, 2011. https://www.psychologytoday.com/blog/canine-corner/201112/phone-sniffing-dogs-new-weapon-against-high-tech-crime.

De Caluwé, Roger. *De Eerste Belgische Politiehonden 1899–1914*. Gent: Uitgeverij KOJ, 1995.

De Nederlandsche Hondensport (The Dutch Dog Sports). Kluwer, Deventer. Editions from 1921 to 1925.

Dijkman, Theo. *Legendary Working Malinois in the Netherlands and Their Historical Bloodlines: A Retrospective on the Last Dutch Decades up to the 1990s*. Hondensport & Sporthonden, 1997.

———. *The X-Malinois in the KNPV Dressage: Top Training with Dogs of Proven Bloodlines*. Hondensport & Sporthonden, 2000.

Engel, Dick. *Jubileumboek*. Utrecht: UDHV, 1964.

Estienne, Charles. *L'agriculture et maison rustique*. Antwerp: Christoffel Plantijn, 1566. In 1640, translated to Dutch as *De landtwinninghe ende hoeve*.

Freedman, Adam H., Ilan Gronau, Rena M. Schweizer, et al. "Genome Sequencing Highlights Genes Under Selection and the Dynamic Early History of Dogs." *PLOS Genetics. PLOS Org* 10, no. 1 (January 16, 2014): e1004016. https://doi.org/10.1371/journal.pgen.1004016.

Germonpre, Mietje, Mikhail V. Sablin, Rhiannon E. Stevens, et al. "Fossil Dogs and Wolves from Palaeolithic Sites in Belgium, the Ukraine and Russia: Osteometry, Ancient DNA and Stable Isotopes." *Journal of Archaeological Science* 36, no. 2, (February 2009): 473–490.

Gerritsen, Resi, and Ruud Haak. *K9 Professional Tracking: A Complete Manual for Theory and Training*. Calgary, AB: Brush Education, 2001.

———. *K9 Complete Care: A Manual for Physically and Mentally Healthy Working Dogs*. Calgary, AB: Brush Education, 2003.

Haak, Ruud. *Belgische Herders*. Best: Zuid Boekprodukties, 1989.

Hansmann, Johann. "Unter welchen Gesichtspunkten erfolgt die praktische Verwendung des Polizeifährtenhundes?" *Zeitschrift für Hundeforschung* I (1931): 14–30.

Huyghebaert, Louis. *Onze Belgische Rashonden*. Magazine Cultura, 1926.

Kraus, Cornelia, Samuel Pavard, and Daniel E.L. Promislow. "The Size–Life Span Trade-Off Decomposed: Why Large Dogs Die Young." *American Naturalist* 181, no. 4 (April 2013): 492–505. https://doi.org/10.1086/669665.

Larson, Greger, and Daniel G. Bradley. "How Much Is That in Dog Years? The Advent of Canine Population Genomics." *PLOS Genetics* 10, no. 1 (2014): e1004093. https://doi.org/10.1371/journal.pgen.1004093.

Lorenz, Konrad. *Man Meets Dog*. Boston: Houghton Mifflin, 1954.

Mynsinger, H. *Puoch von den valken, habichten, sperbern, pfaeriden, und hunden*. 1473. In Max von Stephanitz. *Der deutsche Schäferhund in Wort und Bild*. Augsburg: Verlag des Verein für Deutsche Schäferhunde (SV), 1921.

Pidoplichko, L.H. *Upper Palaeolithic Dwellings of Mammoth Bones in the Ukraine: Kiev-Kirillovskii, Gontsy, Dobranichevka, Mezin and Mezhirich*. Kiev, 1969.

Reul, Adolphe. *Les Races de Chiens*. Brussels, 1894.

Schoon, Adee, and Ruud Haak. *K9 Suspect Discrimination: Training and Practicing Scent Identification Lineups*. Calgary, AB: Brush Education, 2002.

Schmidt, Fridolin. *Polizeihund-Erfolge und Neue Winke*. Augsburg: SV, 1911.

Stephanitz, Max v. *The German Shepherd Dog in Word and Picture*. Augsburg: SV, 1923. https://doi.org/10.5962/bhl.title.118050.

Thalmann, O., B. Shapiro, P. Cui, et al. "Complete Mitochondrial Genomes of Ancient Canids Suggest a European Origin of Domestic Dogs." *Science* 342, no. 6160 (15 November 2013): 871–874.

Vilà, Carles, Isabel R. Amorim, Jennifer A. Leonard, et al. "Mitochondrial DNA Phylogeography and Population History of the Grey Wolf *Canis lupus*." *Molecular Ecology* 8, no. 12 (1999): 2089–103. https://doi.org/10.1046/j.1365-294x.1999.00825.x.

Vilà, Carles, Peter Savolainen, and Jesus E. Maldonado. "Multiple and Ancient Origins of the Domestic Dog." *Science* 276, no. 5319 (1997): 1687–9. https://doi.org/10.1126/science.276.5319.1687.

Zeuner, Frederick Everard. *A History of Domesticated Animals*. New York: Harper and Row, 1963.

About the Authors

Ruud Haak is the author of more than 30 dog books in Dutch and German. Since 1979 he has been the editor-in-chief of the biggest Dutch dog magazine, *Onze Hond* (*Our Dog*). He was born in 1947 in Amsterdam, the Netherlands. At the age of 13, he was training police dogs at his uncle's security dog training center, and when he was 15, he worked after school with his patrol dog (which he trained himself) at the Amsterdam harbor. He later started training his dogs in Schutzhund and IPO, and he successfully bred and showed German shepherds and Saint Bernards.

Ruud worked as a social therapist in a government clinic for criminal psychopaths. From his studies in psychology, he became interested in dog behavior and training methods for nose work, especially the tracking dog and the search-and-rescue dog. More recently he has trained drug- and explosive-detector dogs for the Dutch police and the Royal Dutch Airforce. He is also a visiting lecturer at Dutch, German, and Austrian police-dog schools.

In the 1970s, Ruud and his wife, Dr. Resi Gerritsen, a psychologist and jurist, attended many courses and symposia for Schutzhund, tracking, and search-and-rescue dog training in Switzerland, Germany, and Austria. In 1979, they started the Dutch Rescue Dog Organization in the Netherlands. With that unit, they attended many operations responding to earthquakes,

206 ABOUT THE AUTHORS

Figure 8.01 Ruud Haak with his German shepherd Yes van Sulieseraad and Malinois Google van het Eldenseveld.

Figure 8.02 Resi Gerritsen with her Malinois Halusetha's All Power and Malinois Google van het Eldensveld.

gas explosions, and lost persons in wooded or wilderness areas. In 1990, Ruud and Resi moved to Austria, where they were asked by the Austrian Red Cross to select and train operational rescue and avalanche dogs. They lived for three years at a height of 6000 feet (1800 m) in the Alps and worked with their dogs in search missions after avalanches.

With their Austrian colleagues, Ruud and Resi developed a new method for training search-and-rescue dogs. This way of training showed the best results after a major earthquake in Armenia (1988), an earthquake in Japan (1995), two major earthquakes in Turkey (1999), and big earthquakes in Algeria and Iran (2003). Ruud and Resi have also demonstrated the success of their unique training methods for tracking dogs as well as search-and-rescue dogs at the Austrian, Czech, Hungarian, and World Championships, where both were several times the leading champions.

Resi and Ruud have held many symposia and master classes all over the world on their unique training methods, which are featured in their books:

- *K9 Complete Care: A Manual for Physically and Mentally Healthy Working Dogs*
- *K9 Drug Detection: A Manual for Training and Operations*
- *K9 Explosive and Mine Detection: A Manual for Training and Operations*
- *K9 Investigation Errors: A Manual for Avoiding Mistakes*
- *K9 Personal Protection: A Manual for Training Reliable Protection Dogs*
- *K9 Professional Tracking: A Complete Manual for Theory and Training*
- *K9 Scent Training: A Manual for Training Your Identification, Tracking, and Detection Dog*
- *K9 Schutzhund Training: A Manual for IPO Training through Positive Reinforcement*

- *K9 Search and Rescue: A Manual for Training the Natural Way*
- *K9 Working Breeds: Characteristics and Capabilities*

With Simon Prins they wrote *K9 Behavior Basics: A Manual for Proven Success in Operational Service Dog Training*, and with Dr. Adee Schoon, Ruud wrote *K9 Suspect Discrimination: Training and Practicing Scent Identification Line-Ups*. All of these books were published by Detselig Enterprises Ltd., Calgary, Canada (now Brush Education Inc./Dog Training Press).

Ruud and Resi now live in the Netherlands. They are training directors and international judges for the International Rescue Dog Organisation (IRO) and the Fédération Cynologique Internationale (FCI). Ruud and Resi are still successfully training their dogs as detector dogs for search and rescue, drugs, explosives, and IPO Schutzhund. You can contact the authors by email at resigerritsen@gmail.com.

Index

Abbata van Joefarm, 65
Abella du Forgeron, 50
accelerant detection dogs, 181–82
Airedale terriers, police dogs, 132–33, 144
Ajax du Maugré, 67–68
Akira van het Eldenseveld (Google), 78–79, 173, 189, 206
Alix van het Eldenseveld, 77–79
All Breeds Championship, Netherlands, 71–73, 76, 77, 78, 80
Amiga van Joefarm, 77
ammunition detection, 179–80
Amsterdam, police dogs, 143–45
  See also Netherlands
Andor van de Ijsselvloed, 88–90
Anoeska van het Askaremshof, 76
Antwerp, Belgium, 11–13, 51–52, 115–16, 141–43
appearance
  about, viii–x, 32–34, 98–99
  breed standard (1899), 29, 32, 33
  breed standard (FCI), 98–99
  breeding for character vs. appearance, viii–ix, 19–21, 65–66, 103
  head types, 49
  history, 20–21, 23–26, 31–38, 48, 140
  illustrations of varieties, viii, 25, 49
appearance, color varieties
  about, viii–x, 32–34
  black (Groenedael), viii–ix, 25
  black (Malinois xMH), 30–31, 88–89
  black masks, ix, 29, 33, 35, 42
  breed standard (1899), 29, 32, 33, 35
  fawn with overlay (Malinois), ix, 29, 35
  gray or fawn (Tervueren), ix
  reddish fawn (Laekenois), ix
  standard of one color per variety, 29, 35
  See also black dogs
appearance, hair varieties
  about, viii–x, 32–34
  breed standard (1899), 29, 32, 33
  collarette, ix
  long-haired (Groenendael, Tervueren), viii–ix, 33, 49
  short-haired (Malinois), viii–ix, 25, 29, 33
  wire-haired (Laekenois), viii–ix, 25, 33
Arat, 65
Arco, 72, 77, 78
Arco Perle de Tourbière, 82–83
area search, KNPV certificate, 170–73

Argus, 27
Arras, 88, 90, 147
arson dogs, 181–82
art history, dogs in, 6–7, 9–10, 15–16, 112–17
Arva van Joefarm, 65
Aska, 184
Astra, 89
Astrid, 88
Auguste, Joseph, 27
Australian kelpie, 155
Austria, police dogs, 121–22

Balkus (LOSH 39623), 55
Balkus du Gallifort, 56
Banjer van de Wierickerschans, 77–78
Barry, 88
bed bug detection, 183
Beeldemaker, Adriaen Cornelisz, 13
Beernaert, P., 37, 38
behavior
　breed standard (FCI), 98–99
　owners' preferences, 97–98, 188–91
　pack behavior, 93–96
　social hierarchies, 94–96
　stimulus, 96–98
　wolf ancestry, 4–5, 93–95
　See also character and temperament; working character
Bekaert, L., 55
Belgian Kennel Club, 55
Belgian Malinois. *See* Malinois
Belgian shepherds
　about, vii–x, 25, 69–70
　ancestry, 14, 16
　breed standard (FCI), 98–99
　breeding, viii, 19–21
　FMBB championships, 72
　herding trials (FCI), 156
　KNPV eligibility, 144
　LOSH stud book registration, 33
　matching dogs to handlers, 21–22, 99–101
　regional names for varieties, viii
　working character, 19
　See also appearance; Groenedael; Laekenois; Malinois; shepherd dogs; Tervueren
Belgian shepherds, history (to early 20th c.)
　about, 16–19, 23, 69–70
　in art and culture, 10, 27
　breeding, 24–25
　character and appearance, 23, 69–70
　customs and smuggler dogs, 18–19
　cynology, vii–viii, 23–25
　FCI stud book, 32
　Laeken royal park, 17, 35–36
　police dogs, 117–18, 126–34, 139–40
　varieties, 23
　working character, 16–17, 69–70
　See also Huyghebaert, Louis; Reul, Adolphe; Van der Snickt, M.L.
Belgium
　Belgian Kennel Club, 55
　dog ordinances, 12–14
　dogs in art and culture, 12–13, 115–17
　geese farms, 17
　Laeken royal park, 17, 35–36
　Malinois Club, 31–35, 39
　Mondioring program, 59–61
　police dogs, 18–19, 51, 114–17, 126–31, 140–43, 151–52
　WWI losses, 139–40
　See also Belgian shepherds; dogs, history (to early 20th c.); KMSH (Société Royale St. Hubert)
Bella, 46–47, 53, 135
Benny du Forgeron, 50
Bergeot (LOSH 6800), 45, 50
Bergeronnette, 50
Bergman, Peter, 177
Berkelaar, Cees, 73, 87, 89
Berkers, Theo, 88–89
Berry, 83, 88, 90
Bertelsen, Finn, 80
Beth, 44–46, 50, 53

INDEX

Beullens, Mr., 44
Bica Perle de Tourbière, 84
Bicou, 74, 75
Bila Beau van de Ruisdael, 77–78
Bismarck, 46
black dogs
    black Malinois (xMH), 30–31,
        88–89
    Groenendael, viii–ix
    history of, 26, 28–30
    standard of one color per variety,
        29, 35
    See also appearance, color varieties
Blackie van de Welkom, 57
Block (LOSH 9472), 46, 52–53
Bobby Dog, 138–39
Bobinnette, 53
Boele, J., 147
Bogemans, Mr., 52, 143
bomb detection, 179–80
Book of Hawks (Mynsinger), 112–13
Book of the Hunt (Gaston III/X of
    Foix-Béarn), 113–14
Bos, Mart, 74, 82
Boscaille, 83
Bouvier des Flandres
    ancestry, 14, 16
    breeding, 191
    cattle dogs, 20, 22
    customs dogs, 18–19
    KNPV eligibility, 144
    list of KNPV National Champions
        (1946–2017), 191–200
boxers, KNPV eligibility, 144
breeding
    about, vii–viii, 20–21, 189–91
    German shepherds, 149–50
    history of, vii–viii, 19–21
    KNPV crossbreeds, 145
    origin of Malinois, 37
    owners' preferences for behaviors,
        97–98, 188–91
    pure breeding, 20
    standard (1899), 29, 32, 33
    standard (FCI), 98–99

    standards, 20, 190–91
    working character, vii–viii, 101–3,
        140, 189–91
    See also KMSH (Société Royale St.
        Hubert); mixed breeds
bringsel alerts, 171–72
Bronco Perle de Tourbière, 72, 82–84
Bruinsma, J.W., 87
Bruno, 90–91
Brussels
    Club du Chien de Berger Belge,
        26–29, 32–33, 35
    Club du Chien Pratique, 137–38
Brutus, 76
Buck, 90–91
Buddha, 88–89
Bussenius, Inspector, 123–24

Cabaret, 45, 47, 53
Cabil, 58, 65, 74–75, 77, 86, 88, 91
cadaver search work, 173–75
Capi de la Soierie, 55
Carack, 58
Carlo van Kristalhof, 73–75, 77,
    83, 87
Cartouche, 63, 65, 75
Castor von Kronenburg, 65
cattle dogs, 16, 19–20, 22, 51
cell phone detection, 186–87
César de Grand Rabot, 50
Césary, 52, 53
character and temperament
    about, 21–22, 69–70, 93, 97–98
    breed standard (FCI), 98–99
    breeding for character vs.
        appearance, viii–ix, 19–21,
        65–66, 103
    faults, 97–98, 99, 100
    independence, 109
    matching breeds to handlers,
        21–22, 99–101
    Mondioring eligibility, 61
    owners' preferences, 97–98, 188–91
    pack behavior, 93–96
    puppies, 103–7

"soft dogs" (easily discouraged), 100–101
temperament spectrum, 97–98
"think ahead" ability, 109
working character, 19–21, 85
See also training; working character
Charlois, 25
Charlot, 27
Chop, 46
Cjoe van Joefarm, 65
Clarys, A., 25, 27
Clip (LOSH 412720), 62, 74, 75, 77
Club du Chien de Berger Belge, Brussels, 26–29, 32–33, 35
Club du Chien Pratique, Brussels, 137–38
coats. *See* appearance
Cobra van Tasca's Home, 72
Cody Perle de Tourbière, 84
Coenen, Mr., 135–37
collies
  breeding, 33–34
  British imports, 23–24, 26
  herding, 155
  mixed breed police dogs, 133
color varieties. *See* appearance, color varieties
Cora I (LOSH 6134), 35, 37, 39, 40, 45–46, 50, 118, 135–37
Cora de l'Enclus, 47
Corer, Stanley, 186
Corette (LOSH 8205), 45, 50, 53
Cotte, Marcel, 44
Courtoisie, 45
Couvreur, Edgard, 43, 47
Couwenberg, Mr., 143
crime and police dogs
  cadaver search work, 173–75
  Duwe murder case, 123–24
  history (to 18th c.), 114–17
  Jack the Ripper, 132
  smuggler dogs, 18–19
  See also police; police dogs
Criquette (LOSH 166749), 86
Crombrugge, Mr., 52

crossbreeds. *See* breeding; mixed breeds
crossed Groenendael (black Malinois), 88–89
Crunelle, A., 49
cultural history, dogs in, 6–7, 9–10, 15–16, 112–17
currency detection work, 183–84
customs dogs, 18–19
cynology, vii–viii, 23–25
  See also breeding; Huyghebaert, Louis; Reul, Adolphe; Van der Snickt, M.L.

Daneskjold kennel, 79–80
Danna, Georges, 44, 48
Dax, 50, 138
Dax kennel, 137, 139
De Bast, Mr., 27
De Grand Rabot kennel, 50
De Hallattes kennel, 50
De Heus, Rob, 72
De Jolimont kennel, 49–50
De la Noaillerie kennel, 70
De Laatste Stuiver kennel, 70
De Laveleye, Mr., 53
De l'Ecaillon kennel, 49, 56, 57
De Meyer, Mr. and Mrs., 127
De Mulder, Charles, 28
De Wet (LOSH 6466), 37, 39–48, 50, 53
De Wilde, Marc, 63, 75
Debora, 83
Dekx, 74–75, 77
Delin, René, 49
Den Oudsten, Willem, 79
Denmark, kennels, 79–80
Derks, Wiel, 88, 90
Des Deux Pottois kennel, 62–63, 73
Desire, 58–59
detection work
  about, 157–58, 186–87
  accelerant detection, 181–82
  alerts, 171–72, 177
  arson dogs, 181–82
  bed bug detection, 183

cadaver search, 173–75
cell phone detection, 186–87
currency detection, 183–84
drug detection, 177–79
explosive and mine detection, 179–80
mold detection, 182–83
new tasks, 186–87
oil and gas detection, 184–86
ore deposit dogs, 175–77
training with toys, 177, 179, 182
See also KNPV Search Dog scent work; KNPV Search Dog search and rescue; KNPV Search Dog tracking
Devil van Joefarm, 65
Dhora, 50
Diane, 37, 38
Dianelle, 47
Dianitte, 53
Dick, 25, 27
Dico, 89
Dijkman, Theo
  coach for World Championship, 72
  Fiërro Perle de Tourbière, 84
  "Legendary Working Malinois in the Netherlands," 69–79
  "The xMalinois in KNPV Dressage," 85–92
Dingo (LOSH 8199), 44–46, 50, 53
disaster work. *See* search and rescue (SAR)
Djecko des Bas Jardins, 45–46, 50
Djipsy, 46
Doberman, 144, 191
dogs
  matching breeds to handlers, 21–22, 99–101
  overheating, 108–9
  pack behavior, 4–5
  vision at night, 4
  See also Belgian shepherds; shepherd dogs
dogs, history (to early 20th c.)
  in art and culture, 6–7, 9–10, 15–16, 112–17

breeding, 16
character vs. appearance, 16, 19–21
dog catchers (stick men), 13–14
domestication as pets, 3–5, 12
early dog ordinances, 11–13
farm dogs, 5, 8, 10, 16–17, 19–21, 102–3
history (ancient history), 1–8, 93–94, 112
history (medieval to early 20th c.), 10–16, 112–17
hunting dogs, 16, 112–14
matins (ignoble dogs), 11–16, 115
noble dogs, 10–11
pack behavior, 4
police dogs, 112–17
varieties and categories, 10, 11, 20–21, 112
wolf ancestry, 1–8, 93–94
wolves as predators on dogs, 11, 14–15
working character, 14–17, 102–3
See also Malinois, history (before 20th c.); shepherds and sheep; shepherd dogs; wolves
Dolie des Deux Pottois, 75
Donna, 73, 90
Dracka (LOSH 428286), 67
drug detection, 177–79
Du Forgeron kennel, 50
Duc, 25, 27
Duc de Bruges, 45
Duc du Rupel, 52, 143
Ducassor, 50
Duchenoy, Mrs., 39
Duke, 27
Dupuis, Mr., 44
Durand, O., 54
Dutch Dog Studbook (NHSB), 141
Dutch Malinois
  famous dogs, 67–68, 72–79, 86–92
  famous kennels, 79–84
  history of, viii, 69–70

KNPV police dogs, 70–71
mixed Malinois, 70, 85–92
working character, 69–70
Dutch Police Dogs Association. *See*
KNPV (Royal Dutch Police Dog Association)
Dutch shepherds
about, 18–19
ancestry, 14, 18, 31–32
herding trials (FCI), 156
list of KNPV National Champions (1946–2017), 191–200
police dogs, 51
Duwe murder case, 123–24
DVG (German Association for Working Dog Sports Clubs), 58

Ecapi de Grand Rabot, 50, 65, 75
Eddy Merckx, 86
Educo, 65
Egyptian ancient culture, 6, 112
Eik des Deux Pottois, 72–73, 75–77, 82–83, 90–92
Eindhoven, 68
Elgos du Chemin des Plaines, 62–65
Embrechts, Mr., 137
Engel, Dick M., 6, 8
England. *See* United Kingdom
Eppink, Mr., 88
Eros, 58
Eva, 180
Evelien van de Hoefaert, 67
explosives detection, 179–80
exterminators and bed bug detection, 183

Fabrice, 47
Fally, V., 39, 41, 43
Fany, 50
Farro von Sophienbusch (Rottweiler), 58
FCI (Fédération Cynologique Internationale)
current breed standard, 98–99
KMSH as Belgium's official club, 32
See also herding trials (FCI)

Fédération Mondiale du Berger Belge (FMBB), 72, 78
Fencha van 't Rodolfsheim, 67
Fidèle du Gallifort, 55
Fidirex van Joefarm, 65
Fidos, 50, 54
Fiërro Perle de Tourbière, 84
Fina, 46
Finland, mineral search, 176
firearms detection, 179–80
fires and fuel source detection, 181–82
flammable products detection, 181–82
Flanders Cattle Dog, 20
Flap, 57
Flapy ("Rex"), 87
Flèche II, 45–46
FMBB (Fédération Mondiale du Berger Belge), 72, 78
Folette, 46
Forban de l'Enclus, 47
Fram de Jolimont, 52–54, 56, 118
See also Snap (LOSH 10050)
Fram du Bois de la Deule (LOSH 8297), 44–46, 48
France
Malinois, 48, 57, 70
Mondioring program, 59
police dogs, 128, 130
smuggler dogs, 18–19
Frank, 86
Fraternité kennel, 58
Friga, 46
Frijns, Mr., 83, 88, 90
Frits, 135, 143
fuel detection work, 181–82
fungi detection work, 182–83

Gallais, Jean Francois, 63–64
Gary, 58
gas detection work, 184–86
Gaston III/X of Foix-Béarn, 113–14
G'Bibber, 62–63, 65
Gepken, Willem, 74

INDEX

Gerlach, Robert, 122
German Association for Working Dog Sports Clubs (DVG), 58
The German Shepherd Dog in Word and Picture (Stephanitz), 6
German shepherds
  ancestry, 6, 8, 14, 29
  breeding, 149–50, 191
  herding trials (FCI), 156
  list of KNPV National Champions (1946–2017), 191–200
  matching dogs to handlers, 21–22
  police dogs, 51, 123–25, 149–50
Germany
  Mondioring program, 59
  police dogs, 122–26, 130, 149–50
  training programs, 58
Gerritsen, Resi, 78–79, 80–81, 170, 205–8
Geudens, Gustaaf, 32
Ghent, police dogs, 121, 126–30, 131, 140, 143
giant schnauzer, 144, 191
Gielens, P., 143
Gip, 50
Gladdy van de Purpere Heide, 74
Gladiateur de l'Ecaillon, 57
Glasgow, Scotland, police dogs, 132–34
Google (van het Eldenseveld), 78–79, 173, 189, 206
goose guardians, 17
Grand Prix of Belgium, 54–58
Greek ancient culture, 7
Groenedael
  about, viii–x
  appearance, viii–ix, 25
  breed standard (1899), 29, 32, 33
  breed standard (FCI), 98–99
  character, 52
  demonstrations, 138–39
  famous dogs, 88–89
  LOSH stud book registration, 33
  police dogs, 51, 128, 130, 135–36
  regional name, viii
  standard of one color per variety, 29, 35
  See also Belgian shepherds
Gross, Hans Gustav Adolf, 121–22
G'Vitou des Deux Pottois, 63, 72, 74–75, 77

Haak, Ruud, 78–79, 80–81, 180, 205–8
Hab, 58
hair varieties. *See* appearance, hair varieties
Halusetha's kennel, 76, 79–82
Halusetha's Aico, 82
Halusetha's All Power, 170, 206
Halusetha's Be Speedy, 80–81, 108
Halusetha's Bianca, 82
Halusetha's Bobby, 79–81
Halusetha's Donder, 79
Halusetha's Igor, 72, 74–76, 78, 79–80
Halusetha's Igor Jr., 81
Halusetha's Karma, 81
Halusetha's Mac, 78
Halusetha's Nesch, 79
Halusetha's Pukkie Dulfer, 80
Halusetha's Quinta, 82
Halusetha's Silex, 82
Hanappe, Arthur, 49, 54
Handbook for Magistrates, Police Officials, and Military Policemen (Gross), 121
handlers and owners
  about, 99–102
  matching dogs to handlers, 21–22, 99–101
  owners' preferences for behaviors, 97–98, 188–91
  police dogs, 125–26
  See also puppies; training
Hansmann, J., 125
Hanssen, Henri, 52–54, 56, 143
Hansum, Jan, 78
Harras von der Polizei, 123–24
head types, 49
Hector, 143
Hélène de la Dendre, 46, 53

herding trials (FCI)
  Collecting Style, 153–55
  Herding Working Test (HWT), 156
  International Herding Trial (IHT), 156–57
  Traditional Style, 155–57
  See also shepherds and sheep; shepherd dogs
Herfkens, Mr., 144
Heuvelmans, L., 67–68
history of Belgian shepherds. *See* Belgian shepherds, history (to early 20th c.)
history of dogs. *See* dogs, history (to early 20th c.)
history of Malinois. *See entries beginning with* Malinois, history
Hogeling, J.A., 88
Hoogenboom, Mr., 87
human remains search, 173–75
hunting dogs, 113–14
Huyghebaert, Frans, 27, 40
Huyghebaert, Louis
  cynologist, 24
  exhibition (1903), 134, 137
  founding of Malinois Club, 32
  "Onze Belgische Rashonden," 33, 34, 44, 134
  Ter Heide kennel, 54, 202n8
  views, 7, 29, 33, 35, 66, 118–19
hyperthermia, 109

Ideal de l'Ecaillon, 56, 57
IEDs (improvised explosive devices) detection work, 179–80
ignoble dogs, 10–11
Igor Perle de Tourbière, 82–84, 162
Ika, 71–73, 76, 79–80, 82
Ika des Deux Pottois, 72, 76–77
Inousca, 62
IPO-Schutzhund, 59, 67, 71–72, 79
Ivan de l'Ecaillon, 56, 57
Iwan, 88, 89

Jaks, 143
Jansen, Mr., 86, 88, 90
Janssen, Frans, 72, 78
Janssens, Jan-Baptist, 17, 27, 35–36
Javotte du Bois de la Deule, 45–46
Jensen, Margit, 80
Jill Perle de Tourbière, 84
Joenda, 75
Joepy, 61–62
Joerie, 72–77, 82
Jolimont kennel, 53
Jordaens, Jacob, 12
Jorka, 91–92
Josque, 75
Joubert, 135–36
Jubileumboek (Engel), 6

Kahma, A., 176
Kamps, Mr., 88
Kangal dogs, 11
Kastor van de Rita's Home, 73–74, 77, 89–90
Kazan, 90–91
Kenis, Mr., 143
Kessler, Mr., 144
Khaki (LOSH 10040), 47, 53
Kiener (LOSH 197867), 86–87, 90
Killer (LOSH 14912), 54, 143
Kleinhesselink, Berry, 79
Klotz, P.V.M., 91
KMSH (Société Royale St. Hubert)
  Belgium's official FCI club, 32
  Grand Prix of Belgium, 54–58
  LOSH (stud book), 33, 120
Knap ter Heide, 44
KNPV (Royal Dutch Police Dog Association)
  about, 68–69, 85
  eligibility, 144–45
  founding (1907), 85, 140–41, 144
  mixed and registered Malinois, 70–71, 85
  Mondioring program, 59–61
  National Championships, 68–69, 71
  National Championships list (1946–2017), 193–200
  working character, 85, 140–41

INDEX

KNPV PH-1 and PH-2 and Object Guarding police dog certificates
  about, 68, 144–49
  eligibility, 68, 144–45
  handler's presentation, 146
  list of champions (1946–2017), 193–200
  Object Guarding, 68, 144, 193
  PH-1 test, 144, 146–49
  PH-2 test, 144–45
  protection work, 146–48
  varieties eligible for, 144–45
  water work, 146–47
KNPV Search Dog scent work
  about, 144, 157
  alerts, 171–72
  Scent Discrimination (A and B), 158, 164–68
  sorting boards, 161, 164–68
  See also detection work
KNPV Search Dog search and rescue
  about, 144, 158
  alerts, 171–72
  Area Search (A and B), 158, 170–73
  Basic Certificate search, 158–61
  Rubble Search (A and B), 158, 169–70
  See also search and rescue (SAR)
KNPV Search Dog tracking
  Tracking Certificate (A and B), 144, 158, 162–64
Koos van 't Haagse Bloed, 77–78
Köpp, Erik, 72, 82
Koppehele, Thomas, 154
kruising Melchelse Herder (xMH), 85
  See also mixed Malinois (xMH)
Kyra, 186

Laeken royal park, 17, 35–36
Laekenois
  about, viii–x, 35–36
  appearance, viii–ix, 25, 35–36, 49
  breed standard (1899), 29, 32, 33
  breed standard (FCI), 98–99
  regional name, viii
  royal gardens in Laeken, 35–36
  standard of one color per variety, 29, 35
  See also Belgian shepherds
Lamers, Bert, 72–74, 83, 90–91
Lando, 79–80, 82
Larco Perle de Tourbière, 77, 82–84
Laron, 90
Ledy du Plateau, 55
Leenders, Mr., 88, 90–92
"Legendary Working Malinois in the Netherlands" (Dijkman), 69–79
Lemmers, Theo, 74
Lennartz, Mr., 88, 91
Leon, 87
Leuven, Belgium, 116–17
Lianique's Arca, 67–68
Lianique's kennel, 67
Lili Folette, 50
Linda, 90–92
Linders, Toine, 86
Liske de Laeken, 36–37, 39
Livres des Origines St. Hubert (LOSH), 33, 120
Lokerse, Mr., 143
Lolo de Watermael (LOSH 6805), 37, 43, 45
London, police dogs, 132–34
long hair. *See* appearance, hair varieties
LOSH stud book (KMSH), 33, 120
Loupo, 47
Lucas des Deux Pottois, 65

Mairesse brothers, 39, 41
Major, 50
Malaise, Mr., 55
Maline des Pimprenelles, 57
Malines, Belgium
  first police dog trials (1903), 134–38
  Malinois Club, 31–35, 39
  police dog training (19th c.), 117–21
  See also Belgium

Malinois
  about, viii–ix
  active service term, 22
  appearance, viii–x, 29, 31, 35, 49
  breed standard (1899), 29, 32, 33
  breed standard (FCI), 98–99
  list of KNPV National Champions (1946–2017), 191–200
  LOSH stud book registration, 33
  regional name, viii
  See also Belgian shepherds
Malinois, history (before 20th c.)
  ancestry, 14–15
  appearance, 31–32
  early dog shows (1890s), 25–27, 31–32
  See also dogs, history (to early 20th c.); shepherd dogs
Malinois, history (early 20th c.)
  about, 23–25
  appearance, 33–35
  breed standard (1899), 29, 32, 33
  competitions, 35, 39
  exports to other countries, 130–31
  famous dogs, 35–47
  Malinois Club, 31–35, 39
  origin of, 35–43
  working character, 34–35
  WWI losses, 44, 48, 139–40
Malinois, history (interwar years)
  about, 48–54, 140–41
  appearance, 48, 140
  competitions, 51–56, 140–41
  famous dogs, 49–54
  police dog training, 141–43
  ringsport, 54, 55, 57
  working character, 140
Malinois, history (after WWII)
  about, 56–59
  famous dogs, 61–65, 72–84, 86–92
  Grand Prix of Belgium, 54–58
  Mondioring program, 59–61
  ringsport, 61–62, 67, 102
  WWII losses, 56, 141
Malinois Club, Malines, 31–35, 39

Mandemakers, Piet, 90–91
Marcella, 53
Marco, 88
Marco van de Veldmolen, 73–74, 77
Marcotte, 46
Marcus, Mr., 92
Margot, 50
Marko van de Veldmolen, 73–74, 77
Marpha, 53
Marquise ter Hoven (LOSH 8828), 46
Mascotte, 46
Mascotte du Tigre Royal, 54
Mastock (LOSH 8570), 45, 50, 53
matins (ignoble dogs), 11–16, 115
Mattsson, Pentti, 176
Max, 143
medical detection, 186
Melba, 46
Menneke, 28–29, 30
methane, 185
Meule, Arthur, 25, 27
Milord, 28
Milord de la Clef des Champs, 57
mine and explosive detection, 179–80
mineral deposit search work, 175–77
Minox (LOSH 10043) (Malinois), 49–50
Minox (LOSH 15141) (Tervueren), 50
Miss, 53
Missouri, 65
Miss-Pratique, 138
mixed breeds
  ancestry, 145
  KNPV eligibility, 144–45
  list of KNPV National Champions (1946–2017), 191–200
mixed Malinois (xMH)
  about, 85, 92
  black Malinois, 30–31, 88–89
  Dutch breeding, 70–71, 85–92
  IPO championship exclusion, 71
  KNPV eligibility, 144
  KNPV training, 70–71, 85
  working character, 101–2

"The xMalinois in KNPV Dressage," 85–92
mold detection work, 182–83
Monarque, 54
Mondioring program, 59–61
money detection work, 183–84
Mouche, 37, 39, 41, 45–46, 50, 53
Moucheron, Edmond, 137–38
Mouw, Willem, 154–55
Muller, Mr., 144
Murke, 138
Mustonen, T., 176
Mynsinger, Heinrich, 112–13

Narcilo, 73–74, 77, 87, 90
Nelton des Deux Pottois, 62–63
Nène, 50
Nero, 88–91
Nervien de l'Ecaillon, 56, 57
Netherlands
  ancestry of shepherd dogs, 14, 31
  Dutch Dog Stud Book (NHSB), 141
  famous dogs, 67–68, 72–79, 86–92
  famous kennels, 79–84
  IPO-Schutzhund, 71–72
  police dogs, 140–41, 143–45
  WWII losses, 141
  See also Dutch Malinois; Dutch shepherds; KNPV (Royal Dutch Police Dog Association)
New Year's Greetings of the Night Watchmen, 116–17
New York City, police dogs, 130–31
NHSB (Dutch Dog Stud Book), 141
Nick, 138
Nina, 49–50
Ninon de l'Enclus (LOSH 8209), 43, 47
noble dogs, 10–11
Noël, André, 70, 83
Nopi, 73–74, 77, 91
Novak du Boscaille, 79
NVBK (National Federation of Belgian Cynologists), 86

Object Guarding (KNPV), 68, 144, 193
  See also KNPV PH-1 and PH-2 and Object Guarding police dog certificates
oil and gas detection, 184–86
"Onze Belgische Rashonden" (Huyghebaert), 33, 34, 44, 134
Opdebeeck, L., 35, 37, 39, 118, 135–36
ore deposit search work, 175–77
Oscar "Jalk," 73, 87–89
Osswald, Robert, 58–59
Othar de la Noaillerie, 82–83
Othar Perle de Tourbière, 82, 84, 145, 158
overheating, 108–10
overwork caution, 108–10
owners. *See* handlers and owners

pack behavior, 93–96
  See also character and temperament
Pan des Pimprenelles, 56, 57
Paul, 28, 30
Pecco, 88
Pegge, Mr., 88
Pélo du Bois de la Deule, 47
Perle de Tourbière kennel, 82–84
petroleum detection work, 184–86
PH (Police Dog) program. *See* KNPV (Royal Dutch Police Dog Association)
phone detection, 186–87
Picpus, 54
Piet, 143
Pimprenelles kennel, 49
Pinto, 72
pipelines detection work, 184–86
Pippo, 53
pitbull terriers, 144–45
Pliny, 112
Poen, Nico, 71
police
  Belgian police services, 121–22
  criminalistics, 121–22

customs dogs, 18–19
errors, 125–26
fingerprints, 121
history (to 18th c.), 114–17
photography, 122
police dogs
   Airedale terriers, 132–33, 144
   in art and culture, 112–17
   famous murder cases, 123–24
   first trials (1903), 134–38
   German shepherds, 123–24, 149–50
   handlers, 125–26
   history (to 18th c.), 112–17
   history (19th c.), 117–22
   history (early 20th c.), 121–34
   history (interwar years), 141–43
   Malinois's popularity, 149–50
   mixed breeds, 133
   police uniforms in kennels, 127–28, 130
   specialized dogs, 152
   training vs. demonstrations, 137–39
   See also crime and police dogs; detection work; KNPV (Royal Dutch Police Dog Association)
"A Police Assistant" (Gross), 121–22
Police Dog Successes and Tips (Schmidt), 124
Prins, 88, 90–92
Prinz, 50
prospecting search work, 175–77
protection exercises (guarding and searching)
   KNPV PH-1 test, 146–48
puppies
   about, 103–7
   adult bite inhibition, 94–95
   handler's confidence, 105–7
   orientation to environment, 103–6
   quick learners, 106–7
   rest and sleep, 103–5
   schedules, 106
   See also training of Malinois

Quiqui, 50
Qu'rack du Bois D'Emblise, 79

Raak, 75
Les Races de Chiens (Reul), 26, 31
Rachid de la Fraternité, 57–58, 75
raising a Malinois. *See* puppies
Raky, 53
Rambo, 90–92
recall alerts, 172
rekel (ignoble) dogs, 11–16, 115
Remy-Lea van het Baantje, 75
Réséda (LOSH 10065), 55
Reul, Adolphe
   cynologist, 24–27
   early dog shows (1890s), 25–27, 31
   police dog trials (1903), 135–37
   Les Races de Chiens, 26, 31
   views, 35, 36
Reumon, Mr., 43
Rex, 57–58, 87, 90
Richardson, Edwin H., 132–33
ringsport, 54–55, 57, 61–62
Rip des Trieux, 45–46
Rita, 50
Rita de la Campine, 52, 143
Ritot (LOSH 8306), 46
Robbie, 87
Robby, 72–73, 76–80
Roe van Joefarm, 62, 65
Roelof, Henk, 90
Rolf des Elfes, 44
Roman ancient culture, 112
Rosette, 45, 50
rothounds (mold detection), 182–83
Rottweilers, 20, 22, 144, 191
Roy, 88
Royal Dutch Police Dog Association. *See* KNPV (Royal Dutch Police Dog Association)
rubble search, KNPV certificate, 169–70
   See also KNPV Search Dog search and rescue
Rudo, 90–91

Rudy, 83
Russia, police dogs, 130

Sadi (LOSH 13537), 54
Sady-Lancier, 47
Sahra de la Dendre, 45–46
Sam du Thiriau, 54
Samlô, 37, 38
Samox (LOSH 20606), 54
Santa van 't Skepershoes, 89
SAR. *See* search and rescue (SAR)
Sarah van Veldekens, 56, 57
Satan, 135–36
scent work. *See* detection work; KNPV Search Dog scent work; KNPV Search Dog search and rescue; KNPV Search Dog tracking
Schmidt, Fridolin, 124
Schutzhund. *See* IPO-Schutzhund
Scotland, police dogs, 132–34
search and rescue (SAR)
　cadaver search work, 173–75
　famous dogs, 80–81, 108
　overwork caution, 108–10
　scent work, 157
　"think ahead" ability, 109
　water search work, 175
　See also detection work; KNPV Search Dog scent work; KNPV Search Dog search and rescue
Segers, H., 37, 38
Selleslach, Mr., 58
shepherds and sheep
　about, 14–16
　in art and culture, 14–16, 24, 27, 154
　daily life, 24, 28, 58, 102–3, 154–55
　decline of flocks, 118
　Laeken royal park, 17, 36
　music, 15
　relations with dogs, 102–3
　wolf predators, 15–16
　See also shepherd dogs
shepherd dogs
　about, 23

　ancestry, 6, 8, 14, 16–17
　breeding, 16–17, 19–21, 23–24
　character of, 16–17, 20–23
　handlers for, 21–22
　herding trials (FCI), 153–57
　history, 8, 10, 16–17, 20–21, 23
　KNPV eligibility, 144
　standards, 20
　working character, 8, 10, 20–21, 23
　See also Belgian shepherds; Dutch shepherds; German shepherds
short hair. *See* appearance, hair varieties
Sibelle de Jolimont, 49
Sint-Hubertus (KMSH), 86
Sips ter Heide, 54
Sirol, 65, 74–75, 86
Siska Perle de Tourbière, 84
Sito, 58
Sjoegar van Joefarm, 63
Slangen, Jo, 82, 84, 162
Smeijer, M., 76
smuggler dogs, 18–19
Snake, 79
Snap (LOSH 10050), 53–54, 58, 143
Snap van Bouwelhei, 67
Snap van den Leeuw, 56
Snepp, 46
Société Royale St. Hubert (KMSH). *See* KMSH (Société Royale St. Hubert)
Solitaire de l'Ecaillon, 57
Sophocles, 112
sorting boards for scent work, 161, 164–68
　See also KNPV Search Dog scent work
Speedy, 83, 88, 180
spiked collars, 11, 15
Spitz, 27
Spranger, Mr., 77
Steijns, Mr., 143–44
Stephanitz, Max von, 6, 8
Stoned van de Duvetorre, 64
Stormy van de Drijvershoeve, 83
sulfide ores and search work, 175–76

Supra, 46
Switzerland, Mondioring program, 59

Taquine de l'Ecaillon, 56, 57
Tarsam, 53
Tchop (LOSH 8571), 46
temperament. *See* character and temperament
Ter Heide kennel, 54, 202n8
Terpstra, Klaas, 90
Tervueren
  about, viii–x
  appearance, viii–ix, 49
  breed standard (FCI), 98–99
  history of exhibitions, 52
  pedigree of Minox, 49–50
  regional name, viii
  See also Belgian shepherds
Tervueren Minox (LOSH 15141), 49–50
Thijssen, Mr., 87
Thylla, 135
Tibi, 57–58
Tichelaar, Fred, 72–73, 76–78
Tico van het Stokeind, 72, 82
Tijsseling, T., 84
Tinnemans, Jan, 72, 74, 82–84, 88, 91, 145, 158
Titi des Templiers, 50
Tititte, 44, 46, 50, 53
Tjek, 71, 77
Tjip (LOSH 6800), 50, 53
Tjippo, 47
Tjop (LOSH 6132), 37, 39–46, 48, 50, 53, 54
Tjop de la Brigade (Tervueren), 56, 57
tobacco detection, 186
Tom, 27, 45, 52, 118, 119
Tomy, 37, 38, 39, 40, 45, 46, 47, 50
Toreador (LOSH 9180), 45–46
The Tracking Dogs (Sophocles), 112
tracking work
  in art and culture, 112–13

KNPV Tracking Certificate (A and B), 144, 158, 162–64
police dog training (early 20th c.), 141–42
See also KNPV (Royal Dutch Police Dog Association)
Traf, 74
The Trained Dog, Antwerp competitions, 51–52
training
  cattle dogs vs. shepherd dogs, 22
  demonstration training pre-WWI, 137–39
  Mondioring program, 59–61
  sport training in interwar years, 140–41
  See also KNPV (Royal Dutch Police Dog Association)
training of Malinois
  about, 107–11
  eagerness to learn, 107
  matching dogs to handlers, 21–22, 99–101, 107
  Mondioring program, 59–61
  overheating, 108–9
  overstimulation, 110–11
  overwork caution, 108–10
  physical and mental speed, 110–11
  relaxing exercises, 110
  sensitivity to handler, 107–8
  "think ahead" ability, 109
  See also handlers and owners; KNPV (Royal Dutch Police Dog Association); police dogs; puppies
Tuerlinckx, Mr., 40
Tunisian ancient culture, 9

Ultima de l'Ecaillon, 56, 57
underground cable detection work, 185
United Kingdom
  ancestors of shepherd dogs, 6, 8
  police dogs, 130, 132–34

INDEX 223

United States
  Malinois imports, 47
  police dogs, 130–32
Unok van de Oewas, 88
Urosh van Joefarm, 63–64
Vabil, 58
Vainqueur, 47
Valk, Rob, 65
Van Albada, Henri, 41–42
Van Bogget, Mr., 28
Van Breugel, W., 88
Van Camp, Mr., 43
Van de Broek, Mr., 87, 90
Van de Molenbeek kennel, 58
Van de Oewa kennel, 58
Van de Reep kennel, 57
Van de Steen, C.B., 90
Van de Visch, Jan, 77–78
Van de Want, Mr., 90
Van de Weldom kennel, 57
Van den Hoff, Mr., 90–91
Van den Oudenakker kennel, 67
Van der Snickt, M.L., 24, 26–29, 35, 118–20
Van der Steen, C.B., 90–91
Van der Wal, D., 73
Van Fort Oranje kennel, 76
Van Gele, Nicky, 61, 65
Van het Eldenseveld, 77
Van Hooydonck, J., 55
Van Joefarm kennel, 61–63
Van Kerckhove, Alex, 34
Van Leeuwen, H., 56
Van Oosten, Mr., 143
Van Rossum, Hans, 71–74, 76, 79–82, 90, 92
Van Rossum, Sonja, 72, 74, 76, 78, 79–82
Van Steenbrugge, Luc, 73
Van Steenbruggen, M.M.L., 77
Van 't Haagse Bloed, 76
Van Thiel, Christ, 88–89
Van Vulpen, Mr., 90

Van Wesemael, Ernest, 35, 127–30, 143
Vanhaesendonck, Miss, 39
Vansteenbrugge, Luc, 62–63, 73
Varak, 58
Verbakel, Harrie, 67–68
Verbanck, Felix, 49, 56, 57
Verbruggen, Jean, 25, 27
Verhoeven, Peter, 78
Verslype, Mario, 63, 64
Vindevoghel, Bertrand, 61–62
Vinelle, 75
Vonkanel, Mr., 52, 143
Vos I, 36–37
Vos de Laeken (Vos II), 35–36, 39
Vos de Muysen, 37, 43
Vos de Polders (LOSH 5847), 37, 39, 41, 45–46, 50, 53
Wakefield, George, 130–31
Wammes, R., 89
Wanda, 82–83
Wanna, 53
Wanna II (LOSH 7579), 45–46
Warren, Charles, 132
water work, 142, 146–47, 174
Weckhuyzen, Johan, 63, 64
Weekers, J.H., 88
Willemsen, Mr., 88
Windt, Kamillo, 121
Wintergroen, François, 27
Wip, 44–46, 50, 53
"wolf collars," 11
wolves
  ancestry of dogs, 1–6, 8, 93–95
  in art and culture, 15–16
  pack behavior, 4–5, 93–95
  "wolf blood," 6, 8
  "wolf collars," 11
working character
  about, 19–21, 85, 101–3
  breeding for character vs. appearance, viii–ix, 19–21, 65–66, 103

early dog shows, 28, 51
history of breeding, 20, 69–70, 102–3
history of dogs, 8, 10, 14–21, 28
importance of, 103, 188–91
KNPV police dogs, 85
Malinois's popularity, 191
owners' preferences for behaviors, 97–98, 188–91
See also character and temperament
World War I losses, 44, 48, 139–40
World War II losses, 56, 70, 141

Xante de l'Ecaillon, 56, 57
"The xMalinois in KNPV Dressage" (Dijkman), 85–92
xMH. *See* mixed Malinois (xMH)

Yagus van de Duvetorre, 63–65
Yellow van Joefarm, 65
Yes van Sulieseraad, 206
Ymbertine, 75
Youri, 63

Zède, 47
Zet (LOSH 8210), 54